Our Gun Idolatry

I wish to thank my good friends, Julian Friedman and Lydia Sawyer, who read the manuscript, caught many errors, and made valuable suggestions.

Our Gun Idolatry

• • •

Edward L Alban

ISBN-13: 9781984375124
ISBN-10: 1984375121
Library of Congress Control Number: 2018901694
CreateSpace Independent Publishing Platform
North Charleston, South Carolina

Contents

Introduction

● ● ●

WE HAVE MUCH TO BE thankful for in America. We are the envy of the world in many respects and we are admired. But guns are our shame. America looks like the Statue of Liberty wearing a crown of guns whence blood trickles down over her face every time there is a massacre or school shooting. The world sees us in disbelief, unable to fathom how we would choose to wear such a grotesque head cover.

The Second Amendment is our problem. The NRA has turned this amendment into a holy writ, a New Testament. Its meager lines, widely misunderstood and blown out of proportion, have raised gun rights beyond all reason, trampling on other rights in the U.S. Constitution, denying us the safety to pursue happiness in peace, free of the threat of guns. So varied and so pervasive are the ramifications of the Second Amendment on American lives that allusions to it appear in virtually every chapter of this book. It is that ubiquitous. Wherever conflicts, problems, or gun-related tragedies rear up, they inevitably lead to legal and social dysfunctions that are uniquely American and that trace back to the power that the NRA has wrested in the name of the Second Amendment. This amendment is not just the vague pronouncement from antiquity about militias that we often hear quoted. It has been given new life by two Supreme Court decisions in the 21st Century. I cover these in Chapter 15. Unfortunately, these decisions have not addressed the myriad issues that still cry out for resolution and clarification.

I represent no one but myself. As a retired professor of economics I am going to apply my insights to fight the wrong thinking, the fallacies and the butt headedness of this scourge.

There is room for guns in our society. Outright confiscation of firearms is not what I propose. But I do propose restrictions on the types of guns and where and when they may be used. Americans may keep their handguns and their hunting rifles at home. They should even be able to own and operate the much-feared assault guns, but with significant restrictions. They should not be able to keep them at home. They could fire them to their heart's content only at the firing range. The current situation where military-type weapons are taken everywhere has to stop.

As to the Second Amendment, gun lovers should keep in mind that Americans of another age wrote it –not God –and Americans of our day can reinterpret it, or amend it, or rewrite it to suit our times.

CHAPTER 1

Guns Get a Free Pass

● ● ●

GUNS NO LONGER INVOKE REPROACH in America, let alone outrage. These days a gun can strut out of a massacre flaunting a saintly halo of innocence, with its barrel still smoking while people chant the mantra that the gun is innocent, that the sole culprit is the shooter.

Often after a massacre, the TVs stations replay videos of the shooting, with copious commentary from experts who sit around discussing all aspects of the crime –except the gun. Motive is their paramount concern. Everybody wants to know why the killer did it. Was it madness? Was it hatred? Was the motivation racial, homophobic, or xenophobic?

I watch in despair, thinking to myself: Who cares why he did it? What about the gun? The gun! Could he have killed, so effortlessly and so extensively, without a gun? Since he could not have, why then do we allow so much firepower in the hands of people?

But it is futile to think about reducing guns in America. The gun is untouchable. The gun, which the whole world sees as the killing behemoth in the room, is invisible to American eyes; the gun, which spews out bullets and mows down Americans on a recurrent basis, is not seen as a problem. Those who do see it as problem are resigned to its insolvability as if it were a curse that can't be shaken off.

This has to change. We must overcome this sense of defeatism and unshackle ourselves from this curse just as we did with the cigarette. We can beat this scourge as well. But it will be very, very difficult. It will take perhaps 25, 30, or even 40 years. So, let's get started. Let's do it. That's the call and mission of this book.

Our gun laws. At present our gun laws cover mostly gun purchases and little else. When the gun is discussed at all in those roundtables after a massacre, the concern is whether it was purchased legally. If the purchaser passed the background checks and if he dotted the i's and crossed the t's in the paper work, then he became free to do with his gun as he pleased. If he had evil intent when he bought it, he is now free to carry it out. There are no laws after the acquisition. Society can do nothing until he starts shooting people.

The gun-purchase laws help a little, but not much. In the first place, they are notoriously porous. They do not prevent people from getting a gun. Anybody can bypass the purchase rigmarole and get a gun at a so-called *gun show*. This is a private market setup similar to a garage sale. It involves transactions from individual to individual and as such is exempt from the proscriptions of the law. No questions are asked. No background checks are necessary. This gun-show loophole makes a joke out of our gun laws. Why would a person who could not buy a gun legally bother with a gun store when he could easily avoid the paper hassle, the waiting period and the background check?

People are also able to get parts and ammo through the Internet. In fact, the internet gives them another avenue to circumvent the gun stores. People can assemble an assault weapon part-by-part through the Internet with no questions asked, with no background check and no waiting period. Such weapons exist already and circulate under the law's radar. Because they are untraceable, they are known as **ghost guns.** Finally, as if all the above were not enough, there are also black markets for guns and, of course, the purchase restrictions don't apply there.

Obviously, we need to close these loopholes. This is no way to control gun sales. But, more importantly, we need to get past the acquisition stage, past the gun sale. It shouldn't matter whether a gun is purchased legally or illegally, or whether it was borrowed or stolen. We should still have measures in place to abort, to thwart, avert, or, at the very least, frustrate the guns from killing people after they have been acquired. But nobody thinks of going into that territory for fear of inconveniencing the rights of the gun wielder. Nobody thinks about making things less accommodating for the potential killer. Nobody talks about restricting the types of guns that people can keep at home. Why should ordinary citizens need to have the power of an AR-15 assault rifle at home? What war are they going to? We should do more to make the guns safer. The storage capacity of the magazine should be regulated. The guns themselves should emit signals to warn us of their presence. Safe, smart guns already exist and are not just fanciful oddities of James Bond movies. They could prevent accidents, especially involving children and other cases where policemen are overpowered and killed by their own guns. The NRA, for its own mysterious reasons, has fought the ready availability of these guns. There is much that we can do if we valued lives and safety more than shooting convenience for the gun owners. Finally, nobody asks about the what-ifs that could have prevented the killings.

Here is one what-if that nobody talks about. What if assault weapons were not allowed to be taken home? This alone would have prevented many killings. Neither Adam Lanza, nor James Holmes, nor the San Bernardino killer, nor the Orlando killer, nor many others could have carried out their massacres if they could not have kept their assault guns at home. Why do we allow this? Such permissiveness bogles the mind!

We have to change the imbalance between safety and gun rights and give safety the upper hand. For now I shall merely list some possibilities for future discussion.

- Close the purchase loopholes. Actually, there are bills making the rounds in congress aiming to close these loopholes.
- The requirements for a gun license should be more stringent. Applicants should be required to be familiar with the statistics about gun accidents, homicides and suicides. They should be made aware of comparable statistics for other countries.
- We register cars and motorcycles, why not guns?

- We require liability insurance for vehicles, why not guns?
- Stop and frisk operations should be common to absorb unregistered, uninsured and otherwise illegal guns.
- If we inconvenience smokers by banning smoking in many places and we inconvenience passengers by requiring them to buckle up, why shouldn't we inconvenience gun lovers by banning assault weapons from the home? They could keep a handgun at home, but assault weapons must live at the firing range. Rapid fire assault weapons should be kept only at the firing range, not at home. After all, city ordinances forbid firing such weapons within city limits. If sport is their rationale, they can fire away to their heart's content at the firing range. As to the need for self-defense, who are they kidding? The Supreme Court has allowed them a hand gun at home already.
- Future guns should come with implanted devices that emit signals which divulge their presence.
- There are child-safe devices which should be required in homes with children to prevent the hundreds of accidental shootings by toddlers every year.
- Switzerland is very permissive about guns in many ways, but it is also a showcase of how to own guns and be safe. It imposes sensible controls. Swiss citizens cannot take home the ammo. The Swiss also have gun registration and they keep tabs on the guns.
- Ammunition should be administered by prescription, as if it were cyanide, Rohypnol, or other dangerous substances. You should not be able to get unlimited amounts by the Internet as if it were candy.
- The loopholes that allow ghost guns to be assembled should be closed.
- The guns themselves should be redesigned and rendered obsolete by new ammunition which will be strictly controlled. This could be one way of mopping up the existing guns.

- More and more of the guns should be "smart guns" that can be fired only by the registered person. This is not just a gimmick from the movie Skyfall. Such guns have been available since 1996. They are used in Europe, but the NRA has blocked them here. What gives the NRA such power?
- The rounds a gun can shoot should be lowered so that desperados are forced to reload. In many rampage situations this factor has been a saving grace.
- The legal age for purchasing guns should be raised to 25. A nineteen year old high school student, such as Nikolas Cruz, the killer at the massacre in Parkland, Florida, should not be able to buy a rapid fire weapon.
- Every gun purchaser should sign a consent-form that allows the FBI or local police to search their premises so they can see for themselves the quantity of ammo and weapons an individual keeps at home and under what conditions. If children are involved, the storage of the weapons should comply with the safety measures prescribed by law.
- Put limits on the number of AR-15 weapons an individual can have. Just how many do you need for sport or self-defense?
- No one should be able to buy the arsenal that **Stephen Paddock**, the Las Vegas killer (October, 2017), was able to buy. We should have a computerized registration system that would inform authorities instantly of the nature and quantity of the weapons an individual is amassing. If the gun purchases raised alarm, that in itself should constitute probable cause and automatically trigger a search warrant to inspect the suspect's home –before, not after the killings.
- Our alarm system is deficient. We err in favor of killers. People who see or hear signs of trouble fail to report it. Or, if they report it, the officials who get the message fail to act on it. This happens much too often. There should be parallel channels for reporting danger signals, which should include not only the police, but

also the FBI, a TV station and the newspaper. This would lessen the chance that all four drop the ball.

* What good does it do to gather the data and report it if we lack the laws to act on the information? What good does it do report an unstable individual with mental problems who is violent, if we do not have the ability to confiscate his guns? Only five states have so-called "red flag laws" that enable the authorities to take the gun from such a person. The states are: California, Connecticut, Indiana, Oregon and Washington.

* We need to become more street savvy about the portability of weapons. Killers who sneak their assault weapons into school by hiding them in a backpack or in a musical instrument case should not have it so easy. The time has come to use clear plastic backpacks.

There is much we can do to make the country safer without confiscating all the guns. The gun needs to be front and center in our post-mortems of massacres and shootings and should not get the free pass it enjoys. We need to change our laws, but not in the mealy-mouthed ineffective ways of the past that were edited and cherry-picked by the NRA. We want real change. The current situation is untenable.

CHAPTER 2

Our Real Schism

● ● ●

AFTER THE SHOOTINGS OF 2016 in Baton Rouge, in St. Paul and Dallas, the hot issue has been "Divided America." It is argued that America is polarized by racial, religious, political and economic differences and that these differences are behind our gun violence.

We do have divisions, and some of them may play a role in our gun violence. But the real division is in the schism between gun lovers and the rest of us. The chasm is so huge that it precludes communication across it, let alone compromise and solutions. The gun lobby does not brook any suggestions that interfere with their gun rights. Basically, to them the status quo is tenable. The gun casualties are just a cost that society must bear for their gun rights and gun lovers refuse to give up even a smidgen of that.

The Second Amendment is the source of our problem. The time has come to interpret it sensibly, to amend it, or to repeal it outright. If we could coexist with it, if it were possible to strengthen our gun laws and get around the amendment without repealing it, then fine. That would be tantamount to a de facto amendment of the amendment and I would be fine with that. But if it is necessary to repeal it in order to be able to pass sensible laws that would ensure peace and safety, then so be it. Let's get started.

At present it is un-American to even consider such a step. To criticize it is to go against a major strand of the American fiber. The NRA has used this amendment to hype its own powers by giving it unwarranted significance. But people who know the U.S. Constitution far better than the NRA have called its bluff and spoken out against it in unequivocal terms. Chief Justice Warren Burger of the U.S. Supreme Court excoriated it as "fraud" in a TV interview, saying:

> **The Second Amendment has been the subject of one of the greatest pieces of fraud, I repeat the word 'fraud,' on the American public." 1991. Interview on PBS's** *MacNeil/Lehrer NewsHour.*

The video shows clearly that Chief Justice Burger was indignant about the abuse of power in the name of this amendment. But if he was indignant in 1991, imagine how he would be now after the ready availability of assault weapons and so much blood that has been spilled under the shadow of the amendment.

Strangely, this amendment commands obeisance even from those who have been shot, or those who have lost a dear one to gun violence. They often mollify their criticism of our gun chaos with a preface that pays homage to the Second Amendment, saying in their most John Wayne manner something like: "I am a red blooded patriot and I *believe* in the Second Amendment, but the level of gun violence in America today is ridiculous."

The word *believe* in this context is a curious Freudian slip that reveals what an act of faith this amendment has become. We *believe* in it as something one does not question, as something one accepts uncritically without pondering the limits of its implications or consequences. We just succumb meekly to its power as if it were the oracle of a pagan god that we idolize and fear.

A new Second Amendment should have words to this effect:

> *The right to bear arms is secondary to the peace, safety and well-being of the people. Americans can keep handguns at home. They may even own rapid fire guns, but they may not keep them at home. The place*

for these is the firing range. Congress shall specify the type and quantity of weapons that Americans may own and where and when they may be fired.

Conditions have changed since the Second Amendment was written over 200 years ago. It needs to be amended to be suitable and specific to our day. This will be difficult to accomplish because our schism has two deep gulches. One is the mentality of gun lovers and the other is their attitude.

Mentality. Pro-gun people have a different focus on the gun problem than the rest of us. For the anti-gun people it suffices to see the inordinate number of shootings and gun deaths to know that something is wrong and that guns are the problem. Pro-gun people, on the other hand, see the gun carnage, but they absolve the gun of all blame. We don't have a gun problem, they say. The deaths are caused by bad people, by "the bad guys," or the insane. Their solution is: go after them, but leave the guns alone. Leave things as they are.

Gun lovers tend to have a mistaken view of humanity. They seem to think that what is true for them should be true for everybody. If they can own guns and not kill anybody then it should be possible for other people to do the same. Guns, according to them, are not bad for people. Guns don't turn people into killers. After all, they are the living proof of that. So leave the guns alone. Give guns to everybody. It's all right.

The trouble is that after so many massacres, one would think that gun lovers would accept that humans as a whole –not just those who are deranged –cannot be trusted with guns because guns are toxic. But guns lovers cannot see this. And this is what I cannot comprehend.

Our values are different. If we asked whether guns are worth the price in blood, anti-gun people would respond: No! Guns are not worth it. Peace and safety are the desirable goals. But gun lovers act as if they would rather lose an arm or an eye as lose their gun. For gun lovers the gun and the untrammeled rights that they ascribe themselves under the Second Amendment are non-negotiable birthrights that cannot be parted with. Safety and security will have to be accommodated by going around their guns. They direct us towards the bad people. This intransigence makes it difficult to change our laws. We are forced to implement token changes and pass puny laws on gun sales that make very little difference. The violence continues.

Gun lovers are also delusional about the lethal nature of their guns. They go to extreme lengths to decriminalize their guns, to sanitize them and to render them innocuous. They have brain washed themselves into thinking that guns are innocent tools and believe the bromides that the NRA puts out, gems of wisdom such as:

1. *Guns don't kill people; people kill people.*
2. *A gun is just a tool, like a hammer or a saw.*
3. *Cars are worse than guns; they kill more people than guns do.*
4. *The only way to stop a bad guy with a gun is to have a good guy with a gun.*

Discussion with gun lovers often turns sophomoric and counterproductive. Logic and critical thinking are drowned out by slogans and catchy half-truths such as the above. I devote Chapter 5 to debunking these idiocies.

Attitude. Even more frustrating than mentality is attitude. Gun lovers are not irenic; they offer no sense of solidarity with the commonweal. They refuse to make concessions even if it would help society. The country could be going to hell in a gun basket, but as long they get to keep their guns they don't care. This attitude is reflected by Joe the Plumber, the guy who emerged as a symbol of an ordinary American in John McCain's presidential campaign of 2008. But Joe the Plumber showed his true colors when he published an open letter in the website **Barbwire** in May 2014. His letter was in response to the pleas for gun control by Richard Martinez, a grieving father who had lost his son in the massacre of Isla Vista, California a week earlier. This is what Joe the Plumber said:

I am sorry you lost your child. I myself have a son and daughter and the one thing I never want to go through, is what you are going through now. But, as harsh as this sounds, your dead kids don't trump my Constitutional rights.(*Wurzelbacher, Joe (27 May 2014). "An Open Letter: To the parents of the victims murdered by Elliot Rodger". BarbWire: "*

One would think that a country that has been able to mandate wearing seat belts in our cars and airplanes; that has been able to control where and when we may smoke; that has banned guns from airports, from courthouses and legislative assemblies, would be able to control guns better. Sadly, this is not the case. Not yet.

CHAPTER 3

Voices of Gun Opposition

• • •

IT IS DISHEARTENING THAT AFTER trying so hard and for so long, we have not been able to gain better control of guns in this country. We try hard, but are stymied by the gun lobby. A few weeks after a massacre, we succumb to a lull, to a sense of inertia about the gun problem. We lose the fervor for putting order in our chaos. We recognize that our efforts are as futile as rubbing sticks to make a fire that won't ignite. Politicians are no help. They cower before the NRA. To confront the NRA is tantamount to political suicide.

A Google search for Americans who express anti-gun sentiments reveals hundreds of individuals, institutions and corporations who are protesting more and more openly. The list includes celebrities, politicians, executives, media outlets and ordinary citizens. A sense of frustration with undercurrents of defeatism pervades their words. To see what they are saying, visit:

https://concealed.wordpress.com/2007/11/23/famous-people-opposing-the-right-to-keep-and-bear-arms.

It is not for lack of eloquence, commitment or political power that we cannot bring sanity to our gun mania. Just look at the address by President Barack Obama on January 5, 2016. Google has it. For sheer impassioned golden oratory he has no peer. He is a brilliant thinker and a constitutional lawyer to boot. And, most remarkable of all, he was the President of the United States –powerful, but yet frustrated by the inconsequential progress and shedding tears over the children of Sandy Hook Elementary School. We are under a Greek curse of Sisyphean proportions.

Also powerful is the condemnation of the New York Times. A month before the president's speech, the New York Times fired an impassioned volley in a front page editorial that argued for the banning of assault weapons. This was quite extraordinary as it was only for the second time in the paper's history that such an editorial had been printed. The editorial pulled no punches and took on the ready availability of assault rifles. See: "End the Gun Epidemic in America," The NY Times Editorial Board, December 4, 2015.

So it is not for lack of well-articulated arguments that we are mired in our gun miasma. Nor is it for fickleness or lack of personal commitment. Some of the most tenacious people in the fight are survivors, people who have felt bullets in their own flesh and blood such as James Brady and Congresswoman Gabrielle Gifford.

James Brady was President's Reagan's Press Secretary and was shot with the president in 1981as they came out of a hotel in the capital where the president had delivered a speech. James was shot in the head and became a virtual invalid, but his wife, Sarah Brady, became active in the movement and spearheaded the struggle for the control of handguns which culminated on the passage of the Brady Act in 1993. By some estimates this bill has blocked some 2 million prospective purchases that did not meet requirements. Sarah continued the fight, serving as Chair of the Brady Campaign and the Brady Center to Prevent Gun Violence until her death in 2015. She was a fierce attack dog on the heels of the NRA.

Congresswoman Gabrielle Gifford was also shot in the head while she was out campaigning. She and her husband, former astronaut Mark Kelly, started a political action committee to promote gun control legislation. She has proposed limiting the sale of assault weapons and closing the loopholes that favor gun trafficking.

There are other committed politicians who feel the pain of the gun carnage and are very active against the power of the gun in our land. They are concerned Americans, not all Democrats, who strive for a sane coexistence with guns. Michael Bloomberg, the ex-Mayor of New York City, is in the forefront. He has backed his commitment with his own money by funding the cause to the tune of $50 million.

Then there are also the scholars and researchers who recognize we have a problem. They address it rationally, presenting the facts and the metrics of our gun situation. The masterwork is **Private Gun, Public Health** (2010) by David Hemenway. It is a good thing that I discovered this book only after I was well into this writing; otherwise, I would have been disheartened, feeling that I had nothing to add after that definitive masterpiece. But we all have our own voices and our own perspectives. This work is not meant to be as scholarly and formal. As a solitary independent writer I have no staff or the wherewithal for empirical research.

Finally, I wish to recognize two organizations for their unwavering work to prevent gun violence. They are the only organizations we have around to take on the NRA and countervail its awesome power. Both have recently come into their present stronger forms by merging with previous organizations. The first is **Everytown for Gun Safety**, founded in 2014 and financially supported by New York City ex-mayor Michael Bloomberg. The second is the **Giffords Law Center to Prevent Gun Violence,** an organization which came into existence in 2017 when The Legal Community Against Violence merged with Americans for Responsible Solutions (headed by Gabrielle Giffords). I applaud the work of these organizations and have donated to their campaigns.

CHAPTER 4

Our Choices

● ● ●

ECONOMISTS USE THE PRODUCTION POSSIBILITY Curve to show the dilemma a society faces when choosing between two goods or two competing goals. In the usual exposition society has to choose between national defense and civilian goods. But in this book the goods are:

X, a measure of gun rights
Y, a measure of peace and safety from gun violence

The analysis offers no panacea and shows, in fact, that society cannot have more of both goods, it must tradeoff one for the other. Safety can be had, but only at the expense of guns and vice versa. Table 4.1 below is a numerical representation of the curve that helps us understand its characteristics. In particular, X and Y move in opposite directions. As X increases, Y decreases, indicating that a tradeoff is involved. To obtain more X, you have to give up Y. Moreover, because it is a curve, you cannot exchange X for Y at a fixed rate. To increase X by equal increments, you must give up increasing amounts of Y. The constant rate would apply if the figure were a straight line

TABLE 4.1

Guns	X:	0	100	200	300	400	500	600	700	800	900	1000
Security	Y:	1000	990	960	910	840	750	640	510	360	190	0

For example, if you started at the point (X = 0 and Y = 1000) and you wanted to increase X by 100, the move would cost you 10 units of Y because your Y holdings would drop from 1000 down to 990. The cost of X is the amount of Y that you have to give up.

What if you wanted to have an extra 100 units of X and go from X=100 to X=200? This time the cost of Y would not be 10 as before, but 30 since we would drop from Y=990 to Y=960.

Similarly, to go from X=200 to X=300, it would cost you 50 units of Y and so on. Proceeding in this manner we can see that the cost of X in terms of Y always increases as we obtain more X. The curve embodies what economists call the law of increasing cost.

It also works the other way. If we started on the extreme right where X=1000 and Y=0 and wanted to have more Y, the first 100 units of X given up would get us 190 units of Y. But the second 100 units of X would only buy us 170 units of Y, which means that the cost of X is increasing. We can now proceed to the graphical representation of the tradeoff curve shown in Fig. 4.1

To appreciate the significance of the curvature, draw a straight line connecting the endpoints of the curve. The line will be below the curve as in Fig 4.2 (page 25). This is because the exchange of X for Y along the line occurs at a constant rate, whereas the exchanges along the curve are not constant. This also means that for each value of guns, the curve has a higher value of safety than the line. This will come in handy later.

Why is it necessary to be on the curve? Why not above it or below it? We cannot be above it because all points above the curve are unattainable in the short-run. Such points exist in the distant future when more resources or when new technologies come into being and the curve can shift upwards. In the long run, anything is possible; empires can come and go, radical changes can take place and the curve can shift upward and outward. But such moves require tectonic changes, which could take decades. Points above the curve are not in the cards in the present.

Why not below the curve? This is possible, but it is wasteful. Society could always gain without penalties by moving towards the curve. It

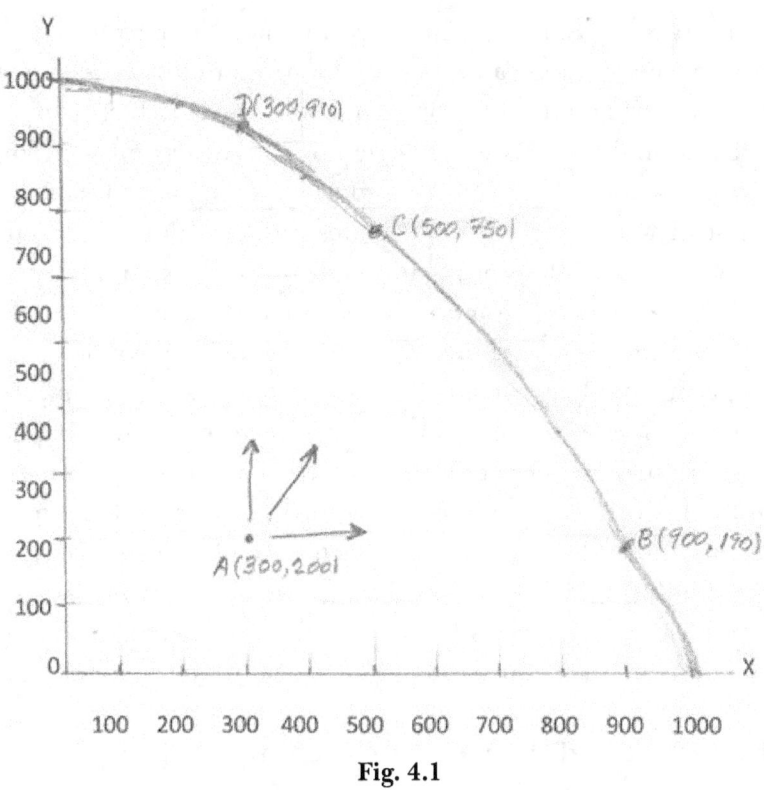

Fig. 4.1

could have more of both goods, or it could have more of one good without sacrificing the other. The move towards the curve would always be a win-win for society and we assume society would always prefer to have more of at least one good if it could. To illustrate the gains involved, suppose society were at point A in Fig. 4.1. From there it could move upward to point D, thus increasing safety significantly without sacrificing any guns. Or, it could move laterally to a point near B where it could have more guns without giving up security. Lastly, it could move to point C, increasing both guns and security at the same time. But once society has used up its slack and reached the curve, further movements entail sacrifices. From that point, the only way it can have more of one good is by giving up some of the other, and this is the implicit dilemma of the

17

curve. Society is forced to sacrifice more and more of one good for each increment of the other because we run into the strictures of scarcity.

Any society, no matter how rich, runs into scarcity. This is the most pervasive and inescapable fact of economic life. Guns and their ammo require steel, wood, plastics and chemicals for the ammo. Safety also requires steel for fences, armored plates and re-enforced structures. Expenditure for X (offense) creates its own set of expenditures for Y (defense). More guns mean more cameras, more alarm systems, detection devices, monitors, bulletproof vests and human resources such as security guards, body guards, policemen, detectives and air marshals. Finally, the competition for resources involves other goods besides X and Y. In particular, security requires battalions of human resources that draw from the overall labor pool of society. All resources cost money and this takes us into budget constraints, which are embodiments of scarcity. In all likelihood peace is costlier than guns, which would mean that the curve is not symmetric as I have drawn it, but asymmetric with an X-intercept greater than the Y-intercept. I make this point in the chapter entitled "Guns Are Cheap."

Where are we on this curve? The curve is hypothetical, but if it were a realistic description of the U.S., I would say we were at point B, on the high end of guns and low on security. To understand how we got there, we need to look at our history.

From the beginning America needed guns. It had to fight the occupying army of the powerful British Empire for its independence. We had to ensure that every colonial, whether farmer, craftsman or trader, could wield a gun to defend the fledgling nation. The Second Amendment was passed for such a purpose. All through the 19th Century the gun served us well. The expansion and conquest of the American West was violent and re-enforced our dependence on the gun. The gun thus became part of our culture. But by the 20th Century we began to realize that a plethora of guns had deleterious side effects which impinged on our safety and security. Power corrupts. Guns confer power on people and corrupt them. Crime –both organized and other –rose to redistribute wealth on its own terms. But it could not have achieved its ends without guns. Guns became a necessary investment for crime, which equalized wealth by force. But this got out of hand and we began to pass laws to get control of guns. It was too late. By the time we started to turn on the gun, the gun industry had become strong and powerful and fought very hard against any encroachment on its business to ensure its own survival.

It has been a struggle to grovel for bits of safety in a country which got addicted to guns. All we have managed to do is to advance to point B, where we are stifled and paralyzed. We are stuck at B, unable to move to another point along the curve because of entrenched political rigidities that have developed since the NRA turned the Second Amendment into an instrument of clout to protect gun interests.

The NRA draws legal and political power from the Second Amendment and treats it as its golden gift from God. It fights hard to protect it. It spends a lot of money lobbying in congress to achieve this. Right now it is in control of the situation politically. Very little can be done to restrict gun rights and enhance safety. That is why it is difficult to trade X for Y and move along the curve. Any time something is proposed in the interest of safety, the NRA runs the proposal through its filter. If guns or gun rights are in anyway restricted, the NRA considers the proposal inimical to its interests and then plays its trump card, the Second Amendment, and calls the proposal unconstitutional. That kills it. Nothing moves. We remain hooked on guns and the NRA is happy.

I don't like point B. I wish we were at point D. But this is just one vote in millions. My mission in this book is to make a case for moving from point B and to persuade enough Americans to bring it about. Most nations of the first world are at a point such as D, with fewer guns and with more restricted gun rights, but safer. How do we move there? To this we now turn.

The Economic Model. My model is abstract. It assumes that X and Y are purchasable items. But how, where do you buy them? What are its prices? The fact is that there are no markets for these goods. You cannot buy gun rights or peace as you would buy shoes or bread and, consequently, you won't find prices for X and Y either. In effect, my model is an economic allegory that uses a fictitious market with fictitious prices to simulate a complex process that is difficult to envision. Nevertheless, the model simplifies that process and captures its essence. In the end it shows us how we got to point B and how we can move from B to point D.

Make no mistake about it. The exchange of gun rights for safety is taking place continuously in the real world through slow and complex dealings that are fought and negotiated politically in state legislatures and Washington. They are bills and proposals that affect the quality of American life with respect to safety and gun rights. It is not a simple process, but the final result is that we end up with a mix of X and Y. This mix is what my model says we bought. Just look at the world around you and you will see the uneven blend of gun rights and peace that we have. Should we exchange some X for Y? Take a page from our recent history. Visit one of our last massacres. Count the number of victims. Do a post mortem. Ask yourself: Where did we fail? What can we improve? What must we do to prevent it from happening again? Then see what restrictions can be applied to get us more peace and safety. To further clarify, let us imbue point B with more realism by describing it in terms of gun rights and safety as you would see it in the real world. Look around you. What do you see? Here are some of the things you will find.

1. You will see people buying AR-15s, or assembling them at home as if they were toys. These guns will be used to mow down children at an elementary school, such as Sandy hook, CT; or at a movie theater such as Littleton, CO.; or the San Bernardino Shootings, the Baton Rouge, St Paul, Dallas and Las Vegas massacre. You will hear a great outcry and much talk to do something about such crimes. But the gun lobby knows how to bide its time. It will start oiling its own machinery of inaction and it will win. Money will flow. Nothing will be done.

2. You will see a domestic abuser who has been reported to the authorities. Restraining orders have been issued. This man should not be allowed to buy a gun. But here is the rub. The man is not a spouse; he is a live-in boyfriend and the state law specifies spouse. What difference does that make? Good grief, ignore the technicality for the woman's sake! Not so fast, says the NRA. That would violate his constitutional right to a gun without due process. So, the man is free to gets his guns. Subsequently, he kills his common-law wife and four others in a rage.

3. You will see an aggressor in another state where the marital status is immaterial; a live-in boyfriend cannot buy a gun. Even so, he gets his guns anyway. How? He finds other loopholes in our laws. He can get guns easily on Facebook, or at a gun-show, or at a bad-apple store. Our purchase gun laws are a joke. Our commitment to effective control of gun acquisition is sham and halfhearted.

4. You will see a third domestic abuser with a long, bloody rap sheet, who has threatened to kill his wife, who broke the skull of his two-year old step-son in a rage, who killed dogs for sport and who was convicted of animal cruelty. He escaped from a mental institution. He was court-martialed and dishonorably discharged from the Air Force. We finally have a baddie so bad that he could not get past the background checks. And yet, he gets his guns and manages to go through the background checks like Mr. Clean. What happened? His record did not make it to the crime data files. It was not reported. People along the way did not take his background or his threats seriously, or they did not care. Benign negligence? Deliberate sabotage? Whatever the reason, this sort of thing happens many, many times. It is not rare at all. Our culture still lacks discipline and conscience for the commonweal. Our reporting system is woefully deficient.

5. You will see another seemingly upright individual with no police record. He is buying an arsenal of rapid fire weapons from

several stores. Nobody is keeping tabs of his purchases. There is no system to catch this sort of thing. He buys his arsenal as if he were buying school supplies without arousing any suspicion. Normally, if we had alert computer systems, someone somewhere along the way would have asked: Where is the war? Why does he need such firepower? What's he up to? But so disconnected are our systems that the man can amass an arsenal and then carry it to a hotel in Las Vegas undetected. Then, from his secure high perch, he can start killing people at a concert.

6. You will see two inmates on a field trip overpower the prison guards. They then wrest the guns from them and killed the guards with their own weapons. This killing could not have occurred if the guards had had smart guns because these guns can only be fired by the guard. Smart guns are not science fiction. They are real and they've been around since the nineties. They are used in Europe. The NRA has been no friend of the smart guns. Its official position is that it does not object to them, but in practice it has dragged its feet on their use. To be sure, there are criticisms about these guns, but these are mostly theoretical. We have not used them enough to judge their merits empirically.

7. You will see several instances of children getting hold of guns and killing siblings, other family members or themselves. People are too negligent and cavalier about guns. Again, this is another example of our cultural delusion about guns, our underestimation of their danger. People don't have enough respect for their deadliness. Here, also, smart guns could have prevented the tragedies.

8. You will see the NRA and state legislatures pushing to have new open venues for their guns, encroaching on traditional sanctuaries such as college campuses and churches on the wispy promise that people need guns for self-defense. Some states have

bought into this. The momentum for more guns in more and more places is a tide that is sweeping the land.

9. You will see the NRA and some state legislatures pushing concealed-carry laws. But why stop there? Why not go for the entire country and pass the reciprocity law by which state gun licenses will be like driver's licenses. They will be good anywhere in the US. Someone who gets a license from a gun-loving state will be able to carry his gun through the streets and malls of a city in a state which is allergic to guns and where its citizens are not allowed such privileges. To deprive the gun-toting visitor from carrying his gun would violate his constitutional right. So, instead, local laws are trumped by the Second Amendment.

10. But you will also see that sometimes common sense imposes itself –Second Amendment or not. There are restricted areas in airports where guns are banned. You will see thousands of people milling about through the concourses. Normally, these concourses would be ideal killing fields for armed deranged individuals. But at the airports you are comforted by the knowledge that there are no guns around. You rejoice in the safety of airports, in the victory over the Second Amendment, in trumping the NRA.

The above scenes support the claim that the country is high on gun rights and low on safety. Ours is a gun culture. We don't think safety. Guns come first. The scenes show us what we bargained for at the market for gun rights and safety and what we ended up buying. We see that we got gypped, that we made a bad purchase –one which is responsible for too many shootings, too many massacres, too many deaths. We can and must do better than this.

While the above scenes flesh out the characteristics of point B, they do not quantify it; they do not provide a metric that would help us assess the dominance of guns over safety, nor do they give a measure for comparing this situation with other points on the curve. But the model will. For example, the model will be able to say that at point B guns rights dominate safety, that guns are 80% above safety. This, in turn, translates to 32000 lives lost to gun violence. On the other hand, at point D society values guns some 40% below safety. Gun deaths are correspondingly much lower at D, being 12800.

Let us then proceed to the model. The next step is to develop parameters that serve as proxies for the prices of X and Y, thus:

s is the unit value of safety, a proxy for Y's price
g is the unit value of gun rights, a proxy for X's price

Fortunately, it is not necessary to come up with dollar figures for these proxies. It doesn't matter one whit whether they are measured in dollars or euros, or whether they are expressed in percentages or whole values. As we shall see, the model requires only the ratio g/s, which cancel out any denominations. This ratio measures the importance of guns over safety; it quantifies our preferences and places us in our corresponding point on the curve. As we shall see, it also moves us from one point of the curve to another when it changes. The prices enter society's budget in the usual way, thus:

1. $B = sZ + gX$, where B is the budget

Here Z is the amount of safety that society could afford to buy after contracting for X units of gun rights. This measure of safety derives from the budget process whereas Y derives from the production possibility curve. Solving this for Z we obtain the budget line:

2. $Z = B/s - (g/s) X$

Notice that it is the source of the ratio (g/s), which is, in fact, its slope. To further illustrate the significance of this line, let's simplify it further by supposing that society valued guns and security equally so that $s = g$

= 0.5. Suppose, in addition, that B = 500. Then Equation 2 would reduce to this very nice simple line:

3.   Z = 1000 – X,

Equation 3 is graphed in Fig 4.2 below. Through this equation X is exchanged for Y at a constant, one-to-one rate. Each increment of X brings about an equal decrease in Y. This, however, is not the case with the production possibility curve where the exchange of X for Y varies from point to point and is given by the following quadratic:

4.   Y = 1000 – 0.001X²

This function, by the way, is the one I've been using all along, the one that generated the numbers in Table 4.1 and the one that generated the curve in Fig. 4.1. it is redrawn in Fig. 4.2 along with Z.

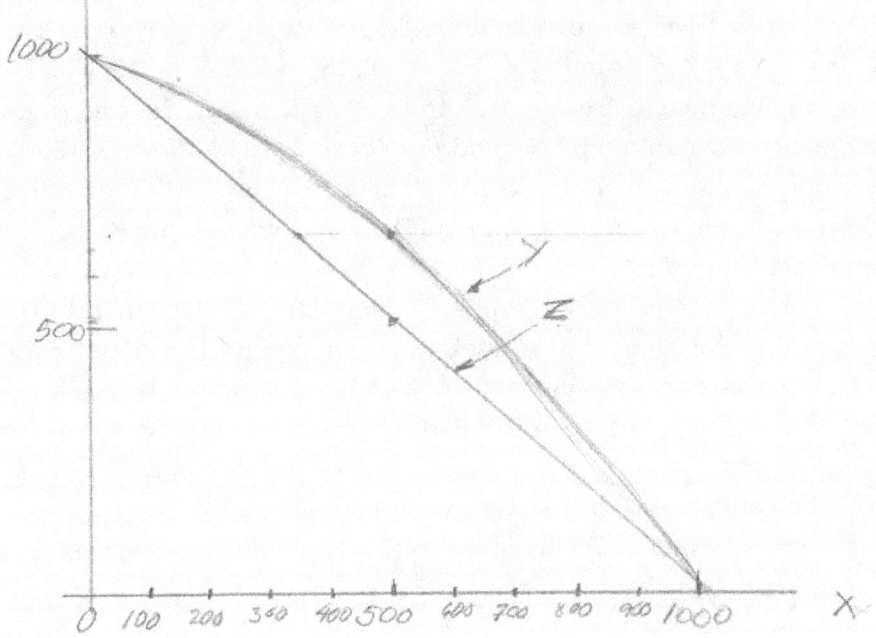

Fig. 4.2

The difference between the linear budget line and the production exchange generates a gap, a benefit to society. It is this benefit that we want to exploit. As Fig. 4.2 shows, the gap is widest at X=500. At that point society can split its budget 50-50, with 500 going to guns and 500 to security. Table 4.2 below shows the numerical values for all the variables involved and identifies the values for points D, C and B.

TABLE 4.2

				D		**C**				**B**	
X:	0	100	200	300	400	**500**	600	700	800	900	1000
Y:	1000	990	960	910	840	**750**	640	510	360	190	0
Z:	1000	900	800	700	600	**500**	400	300	200	100	0
Y – Z:	0	90	160	210	240	**250**	240	210	160	90	0

To see how this table works, begin by choosing a value of X, then drop down to the corresponding value of Y, Z and (Y-Z) below it. For example, if society opted to have X = 200. The curve would yield Y=960, but the cost-driven value of these would be only Z = 800, giving us a net gain of (Y-Z) = 160. Similarly, if X = 300, the net gain is 210. The last row (the net benefit) rises at first from 90 to 160, then 210 and so on; it reaches a maximum of 250 and then declines. Therefore, X =500 is the optimum that maximizes society's net gain. The rest of the optimal figures are shown in bold font. In effect, society has chosen point C on Fig. 4.1.

The sense of the word "optimum" to describe point C is strictly mathematical and economic. It is not optimal in a moral or societal sense, because it says nothing about the cost of lives, the waste, the pain and suffering, the angst of American daily life due to the killings with guns. Those are related but separate issues that have not yet entered the analysis. They will be considered in the next section.

Besides being mathematically optimal, point C also serves as a benchmark. It enables us to gauge other points on the curve in terms of it; it tells us how far from parity the other points are. To see this, let us write the chosen value of X using s and g, thus:

5. $X^* = (g/s)500$

So that when g = s, we have point C and X* reduces to 500. But if we did not have parity, if guns were overvalued relative to security, the ratio would be above unity, (g/ s) > 1. This would shift the value of X* to the right. For example, if g=0.9 and s=0.5, the ratio would be g/s = 1.8. This would increase guns to X* =1.8(500) = 900, putting us at point B, which describes the current point for the US, with more guns than C and less safe.

The fact that g is some 80% above s, quantifies how much we value gun rights over safety. The ten scenarios I presented earlier gives us a picture of what this ratio represents, of what we are living currently. We are quantifying what we are living; we are looking at eighty-percent gun dominance over safety and it is unacceptable. In the next section I will show that it translates to 32,000 gun killings per year.

Let us see what would happen if, instead, people valued security more than guns. In that case, the ratio g/s would fall below unity, and X* would move to the left. People would opt for fewer gun rights and greater security. Specifically, if g=0.3 and s=0.5, so that g/s = 0.6, then X* would drop to X*=0.6(500) = 300. This would put us at point D, where most of the civilized western powers are. At this point one could say that guns are valued some 40% below safety. Gun deaths would be much lower, comparable to those of other civilized western countries which are shown in Chapter 10. The model will also give an estimate for the number of gun deaths for point D in the next section.

In conclusion, every point on the curve is accessible by appropriate values of g and s. The ratio g/s is the critical determinant of our position on the curve. To move from one point to another, society has to change this ratio. Of course, this is easy to do on paper, but not in the real world. These parameters change only when the American people change their values about safety and guns and they take a long time to move inches. But if they ever changed and the change persevered, it would lead to real changes in our quality of life. It would happen like this. We would elect representatives to the House and Senate who would support the people's values and who would fight to change the laws. This is a big order that will not happen overnight. However, once the process got started and Americans began to value safety more than guns, the ratio g/s would start dropping. The transformation into a safer country would start when g/s drops below unity. Many laws would change then, including perhaps the Second Amendment itself.

We are not ready for that yet. Americans still need to do much soul searching, much introspection and philosophizing about guns and safety. Much of what passes for gun rights is nothing more than convenience for gun owners. Right now the Second Amendment is a major impediment because it demands total convenience. Any restriction, any inconvenience is considered an infringement of their gun rights, which is –lo and behold! –deemed to be unconstitutional. That trumps everything. It doesn't matter that this convenience is deadly, that it costs thousands of lives.

The Second Amendment prevents the simplest and most common-sensical solutions to our impasses: be it in the elimination of the boy-friend loophole, or banning gun possession due to grandfather clauses, or stipulating gun requisition statutes, or trumping state and local laws through a country-wide concealed-carrying right, or using more smart guns, or banning rapid fire weapons from the homes, or eliminating gun-show and bad-apple loopholes. The range of our legal disarray is enormous because the Second Amendment is so ubiquitous, so encompassing that it stands before every avenue towards change, blocking action. The solution to our problems seems simple when you view it in terms of the things that must change and there are only two fundamental things, s and g. But they are as hard to move as heaven and earth.

Connection with Gun Deaths. Ultimately the model has to go beyond the characterization of exchanges and points on a curve and delve into their implications in terms of human suffering and social dysfunction. The ideal variable for this is death by guns. Table 4.3 shows how X and Y determine that. The numbers in the table are generated by this equation:

6. Deaths = 32000 + 20(X − 900) − 10(Y- 190)

TABLE 4.3 GUN DEATHS

X	Y	Const	+20(X -900)	- 10(Y – 190)	DEATHS	
1000	0	32000	+2000	+1900	35900	
900	*190*	*32000*	*0*	*0*	*32000*	B
800	360	32000	-2000	-1700	28300	
700	510	32000	-4000	-3200	24800	
600	640	32000	-6000	-4500	21500	
500	750	32000	-8000	-5600	18400	C
400	840	32000	-10000	-6500	15500	
300	910	32000	-12000	-7200	12800	D
200	960	32000	-14000	-7700	10300	
100	990	32000	-16000	-8000	8000	
0	1000	32000	-18000	-8100	5900	

I posit that gun deaths are directly related to guns and inversely related to safety. Specifically, equation (6) stipulates that as we move leftward from point B, each one-unit reduction in X reduces gun deaths by 20, while each one-unit increase in Y reduces it by 10. Therefore, since X decreases by 100 units, this lowers gun deaths by 2000 each time. However, as we move leftward from point B, Y increases –but by different amounts which lower gun deaths by multiples of 10. Point B is italicized and marks the point of departure. Points C and D are also identified for reference.

The constant 32000 in both the equation and the table is the number of gun deaths in the US for 2010, which is the latest year for which I have data. The exact number is 32,163 (cited on page 86), but rounded here to simplify things. This also represents the number of annual deaths for point B, our point of departure. As we move from this point, gun deaths either increase or decrease. They increase if we move to the right (more guns) and they decrease if we move to the left (fewer guns).

It is important to use figures, even if they are only hypothetical, because they help us grasp the logic and the mechanics of the model. I stand by the model's incontrovertible assumptions that fewer guns rights and greater measures of safety reduce gun deaths. The numerical factors –the 20 for X and 10 for Y –are defensible only as guesstimates for illustration purposes.

CHAPTER 5

Idiocies about Guns

● ● ●

No INTELLIGENT DISCUSSION IS POSSIBLE unless we pay attention to what we say and we stand ready to defend our allegations. It is fitting to begin by clearing up the noise of slogans, of inane sound bites, catchy phrases, half-truths and unproved claims about guns. This is the sort of talk which is good for bantering, when you say things for laughs or you try to appeal to the unthinking ones in the crowd. Here are some examples of what I am talking about.

* *My Gun Rights at all costs.*
* *Guns don't kill people. People kill people.*
* *A gun is just a tool, like a saw or a hammer.*
* *If guns kill people, then spoons make people fat.*
* *More people are killed by cars than by guns.*
* *The more guns, the better.*
* *Citizens need to be armed to prevent tyranny by big government.*
* *The only way to stop massacres is to have a good guy with a gun kill a bad guy with a gun.*
* *Guns are cruel, the electric chair is not.*

Guns are nothing to be frivolous about –not when gun deaths exceed 30,000 year after year with countless more wounded. We cannot minimize the lethality of the gun; we cannot rid guns of their morbidity with silly palliatives that cannot withstand scrutiny.

Perhaps frivolity is not the issue. Maybe the slogans are not meant to be funny. Perhaps gun lovers really believe in the shallow logic of these statements and accept them as part of their credo, as part of the arsenal of defenses and rationalizations about guns. If this is the case, then all the more reason they should be debunked. These slogans give false support to guns and, as such, are dangerous.

MY GUN RIGHTS AT ALL COSTS

Law-abiding gun lovers point out that millions of them use their guns for sport or self-protection and not to kill people. Only a few use their guns to kill and thus jeopardize the gun rights for all. Why should so many give up so much because of a few? The good gun owners demand that society go after the criminals and leave their guns alone.

The argument has several flaws. First, we cannot curb the criminals' misuse of guns without restricting gun rights for everyone. Second, the good versus bad dichotomy does not give the full picture. Where do the victims of gun violence figure in this? Third, the priorities are wrong because they weigh human lives against inconveniences. The gun owners are inconvenienced, but this does not rise to the level of a constitutional infringement. Gun lovers can still buy their guns, or keep them if they already have them. See page 3 for a detailed list of some of the specific measures we could adopt.

Assuming those measures were in place. Let us show what they could do. Let the number of non-aggressive gun owners be M millions and let the number of gun-toting criminals be just 3000. Suppose 1200 of the 3000 killers succeed at killing, 700 try and fail, while 1100 hold their guns idle as in the following table.

	Gun Owners	
	Killers	**Non-killers**
Try & Succeed at killing	1200	0
Try and Fail	700	0
Don't try	1100	M
	3000	M

Interestingly, the millions of non-aggressive gun owners play no role here. Their millions are irrelevant since they are not involved in the killings, all of which raises the question: why, then, should they have a voice on the matter of gun rights in the first place? It is true that they would be inconvenienced, but they will not be disarmed. They will have to register their guns, and they will have to keep their rapid fire weapons at the firing range, not at home. That's the extent of their sacrifice.

Here is the real damage report. If each massacre had on average 13 victims, then the total number of victims, V, would be V = 1200x13 = 15,600 per year. This is the figure we should focus on. It is numerically insignificant when compared to the M millions, but the M millions are about guns for sport and self-defense, whereas the 15,600 are human lives. Now consider how the stricter gun laws could reduce the fatalities without infringing on the M million gun users. Here is a before and after comparison which is, admittedly, hypothetical.

	Before Gun Restrictions	After Gun Restrictions
Succeeded at killing	1200	800
Failed at killing	700	900
Didn't try	1100	1300
	3000	3000

First, the number of potential killers remains at 3000 before and after. Successful killing attempts drop by 400 –from 1200 to 800; failed killings rise by 200; while the number of discouraged killers rises by 200 from 1100 to 1300. These marginal reductions produce remarkable improvements in lives saved.

Because killers are forced to use less sophisticated weapons, the number of victims per attempted massacre comes down. The enforcement of the laws closes the easy access to guns and frustrates the killers. Some would resort to stealing weapons, enhancing their risks at getting guns.

If we assume that, on average, each massacre had seven victims, the total number of victims would be reduced to: 800x7 = 5600. This is a significant reduction of 10,000 victims, down from 15600.

The figures are hypothetical. You are welcome to change the numbers to suit your own scenario. But, logically, they could not change the basic outcome which is based on the premise that less weapons in the hands of criminals, that more frustrated and aborted killings and that fewer AR-15s would result in lives saved, whatever the numbers.

GUNS DON'T KILL PEOPLE. PEOPLE KILL PEOPLE.

The first sentence is patently false, like saying fire doesn't burn. One is hard-put to think of instances when it could possibly apply. Would the person who makes this claim dare to taunt a firing squad claiming guns cannot harm him? "Ha, I am safe. You can't kill me because guns don't kill people." Or would he use it to console the relatives of someone who died gunned down by telling them the guns didn't do it? "The guns had nothing to do with it. Honestly. Guns don't kill people."

Guns do kill people! Guns kill, even in situations when there is no willing human killer involved, thus refuting the implied claim that only people kill people. Guns kill when there is no premeditation, no malevolence and no motivation whatsoever, as when a child gets hold of a gun and discharges it accidentally killing a baby sibling; or you lose your balance and drop a gun and it goes off, killing a loved one you didn't mean to kill; or you mistake a hunter for a deer; or you shoot an innocent bystander while trying to hit an assailant; or you horse around thinking that the gun is not loaded, but it is. These things happen often. So, although guns may have no grudge or malice, they do kill, virtually by themselves, even when there is no deliberate human intent.

But if guns can kill when there is no evil intent, think of what they can do when there is hatred, wickedness, malice and premeditation. In these cases the gun becomes an extension of the perverted human who wields it. There is no distance between the man's finger and the trigger. Man and gun act as one, fusing flesh, muscle and metal into a single killing entity. The gun then fulfills its own destiny, its own reason for being, which was killing people.

Long before the killer even thought about killing, the gun was ready to kill, because a gun carries the work of many ghosts in its history, from the inventor and designer to manufacturer, to the dealer and ultimately to the shooter. They all contributed to its final purpose so that by the time the gun is schlepped to the killing scene, it is practically alive, eager and super ready to start killing.

A gun does not need to have a reason to kill. The will, the intent and the malice are provided by their partner, the human killer. But the two together, the killer and the gun, collaborate in an indivisible and inextricable way. It is nonsense to try to deny their joint involvement and try to pin the killing solely on the human. Man and gun together kill. This is so obvious, so undeniable, that we have to ask: Who is trying to separate the role of man and gun? The NRA is –the NRA and all the people of their persuasion. They desperately try to absolve the gun of all blame; they try to exonerate it and purge it of all malice. They want to believe the lie that a gun is as innocent as a tool, as a hammer or a saw.

It happens that deaths by gunfire in the United States have been running in a range from 30,000 to 33,000 persons per year. For those who still have difficulty seeing the gun's inseparable role in killings, I have one final question. Can you conceive of that many gun deaths –33,000 per year, if they had to do them without guns? Could they have killed even half that many people without guns? By contrast, in Japan, where guns are very strictly controlled, deaths by gun are less than ten. Year after year they are in single digits and often zero.

People kill people. This is the remaining vacuous clause which, while true, still sounds dumb because it resonates with incompleteness. An echo barks back: Yes, people kill people, but how? With what? When? Where? Why?

The missing questions are important. It makes a big difference whether people kill others in war, or whether they kill in self-defense, or in the heat of passion, or by accident, or for no reason at all other than the fun of killing, or whether they use knives, or handguns as opposed to automatic assault weapons. It is important to know who is doing the killing and in what numbers. Is it just bad people doing the killing? If so, do we have more bad people than the rest of the civilized world? The statement "People kill people" is cryptic and shallow to the point of being stupid.

That people kill people we have known since Cain killed Abel. That's nothing new. Killing is part of the human condition and it comes in all forms. We have murders, executions, suicides, matricide, patricide, fratricide, self-defense and war. I accept these facts. I am not a pacifist. I am not in some quixotic quest to do away with all killings. I take wars in stride and, for what it is worth, I support the death penalty. The elimination of killings is not what this is about.

Killings will exist as long as humans roam the earth. But accepting this inevitability does not mean that we should abet it and inundate our land with guns that are deadlier and deadlier each year. Precisely because we know that people will kill people we should endeavor to control their killing potential. Putting guns in the hands of more people does just the opposite.

Americans are killing themselves in numbers that surpass significantly the killings of other civilized countries. This is happening because we are using guns –not knives, or bows and arrows. That's the issue.

Finally, bad people and killers are everywhere. We do not have a monopoly of that in America. We cannot solve the problem by turning the bad people into good people. But we can see to it that our bad people don't get hold of guns. They should not be able to keep assault weapons at home and carry them undetected. They should not be able to get their weapons at gun-shows, at bad apple stores or through the Internet and so on.

We can forget about turning bad people into good people. Improvements in religion, education, or economic conditions at our stage of development would have very minimal effects. We are already a God-loving country; we are already an economic power house; we are already among the most civilized countries on earth. And yet we have the scourge of gun massacres. It is not for a lack of religion, or a high standard of living or a high level of education that killings by guns are excessive in America. It is because we make it much too easy for Americans to use guns to kill people. That is why guns are the issue.

Guns –and not thin air –enable people to kill others in greater numbers and at a faster rate than with sticks and stone. The attempt to take the guns out of the discussion by saying that **only** people can kill, and that guns cannot, is just a canard, a disingenuous ruse. I revisit this issue in more depth in Chapter 6: On the Innocence of Guns.

A GUN IS JUST A TOOL, LIKE A SAW OR A HAMMER.

Here is another attempt to decriminalize guns and sanitize them, to confer upon them the innocence of common household items such as a carpentry tool. But this is quite a stretch. Most people cannot warp reality that much.

The trouble is that guns do not have the smell of wood and sawdust of carpentry tools. Guns smell of blood and death. Carpentry tools, except in rare cases, are harmless because their function and their purpose are harmless. But the gun for the most part has no other major function than to kill. If gun lovers insist on calling a gun a tool, they should call it a killing tool. It is not innocent, like a hammer or a saw.

Because guns are killing tools they have psychological powers that carpentry tools don't have. They can change human behavior, terrorizing the unarmed into trembling lambs and the gun wielder into lord and master with the power of life and death over others. The gunman can give orders and confiscate what is not his. In a tense situation this power can bring out the monster in him and can easily lead to tragedy. The margin of error is too small with a gun. The distance from the trigger to murder is too short. A gun changes human dynamics and can change behavior like no ordinary tool.

Guns can poison the ambience, inflaming passions. A verbal confrontation can raise the stakes, rushing forth the adrenalin of both parties. If they are both armed and they know it, the situation can escalate into a shooting war. The fear of being shot first brings in the law of the Wild West where the fastest draw wins and survives. It's him or me. Everybody is trigger jittery.

This charged atmosphere accounts for the high number of shootings by police officers in the U.S. In other countries where guns are not so rampant the police need not carry guns. The risk for being unarmed is low. But that would not work here in the streets of gun-saturated America. The police have to work in a gun-saturated environment, virtually a war zone, where control is tested to the limits of human restraint and results in errors of judgment that produce tragedy.

No ordinary tool, no hammer, no saw can charge the atmosphere this way. Only guns have this sinister power.

IF GUNS KILL PEOPLE, THEN SPOONS MAKE PEOPLE FAT

This is an attempt to make the gun as innocent in killing people as the spoon in making people fat. It is stupid because the antecedent has nothing to do with the consequent. Whoever came up with this needs a basic lesson in if-then propositions. Here are some valid ones:

> If the sun is straight up, then it is noon.
> If X is the father of Y, then X is a man
> If the square root of a number is 7, then the number is 49
> If the area of a square is 64 sq. in., then its sides are both 8 inches long

Whoever came up with this gun/spoon equivalence meant, perhaps, to compare two absurdities, like this: "It is as absurd to say that guns kill people as it is to say that spoons make people fat." But the trouble with comparing absurdities is that anything goes. One could just as well say: "It is as absurd to say that guns do **not** kill people as it is to say that spoons make people fat."

Guns are dangerous instruments of death and all the loopy commentary about what spoons can and cannot do won't change that.

MORE PEOPLE ARE KILLED BY CARS THAN BY GUNS.
This statement is true, if you compare totals. However, the comparison of totals is flawed because they include things which are incommensurable. Only a fool would compare car accidental deaths with homicides. These are entirely different things. The rational comparison is as follows:

accidental deaths by cars with accidental deaths by guns
suicides by car with suicides by gun
murders using cars with murders using guns

When the comparison is carried out sensibly it robs the bluster out of the statement and, interestingly, the guns do not fare so well against cars.

It is true that car fatalities are huge: 32,885 in 2010 and, in fact, are slightly greater than gun fatalities as the table below shows. But practically all car deaths were accidental, non-intentional and without premeditation. The qualifier "practically" is necessary because some of the deaths could have been suicides or homicides. Occasionally deranged individuals ram their car into a crowd in order to kill them. Sometimes people do commit suicide by running off a cliff or crashing into a concrete abutment at 90 miles per hour. But most often we cannot tell their intent with certainty.

This is the reason for the question marks in the table. In the case of carbon monoxide poisoning using a car we are able to say that it was apparently suicide. But in the case of car wrecks, the circumstantial evidence at the wreck scene ordinarily points to accidents. Deaths by guns on the other hand do leave indications which point to homicide or suicide. In some cases there are suicide notes, or there is an apparent motive, or there are other forensic data which indicate that the deaths were not accidental.

DEATHS FOR 2010

	ACCIDENTAL	SUICIDE	HOMICIDE	TOTALS
CARS	32,885	?	?	32,885
GUNS	606	19,392	11,078	31,077

Source: http://smartgunlaws.org/gun-deaths-and-injuries-statistics/

Over 30,000 of the gun fatalities were killings, either homicides or suicides. Accidental deaths by guns were comparatively miniscule, 606.

Accidents are, by definition, fortuitous events without the bane of malicious intent. If all gun deaths were by accidents, guns would not be the scourge that they are and we would not have a gun problem. The number of accidental gun fatalities –606 out of a population of 312 million –is so miniscule as to be a cause for celebration. Hurrah! No murders. No suicides. I would personally pop out the champagne and toast the NRA.

But fatalities, even when they are accidental, are a cause for concern. When car deaths reach the staggering number of over 30,000 persons year after year, they are intolerable, totally unacceptable. Such a hefty statistic cannot be dismissed as unavoidable and accepted nonchalantly. We have to examine the cause of so many accidents and come up with ways to reduce their number. That we have done. We have been aggressive about this. We have imposed controls and mandated safety measures to the manufacturers and they have complied. In the case of cars, there is no NRA, there are no major impediments. Here are some of the factors and players involved in vehicular control and safety.

Car manufacturers work hard at ensuring car safety.

Governments maintain the infrastructure of roads, overpasses, exits ramps, bridges, tunnels and railroad crossings.

The media inform the public on all developments in the above.

Drivers have to be licensed to drive. They must demonstrate competence.

Laws are constantly updated, banning DUI, chatting on the phone, not wearing seat belts, texting, speeding, recklessness, operating a vehicle without a driver's license or without liability insurance.

Police enforce the above laws and provide assistance.

Courts mete out justice and award compensation to victims from irresponsible drivers.

The degree of controls is extensive; the commitment to safety by all the aforementioned is total. The efforts have been fruitful. Deaths by car now grow at a slower rate relative to population and miles driven. It is much easier to be proactive with cars than it is with guns. We are able to pass legislation to control all aspects of driving. This is not possible with guns because the gun lobbies often block changes which they consider infringements on their gun rights. When it comes to the car, we do not have impediments from lobbies that wrap themselves around a Second Amendment for Cars. Manufacturers may resist at first and they may delay the implementation of certain measures, but in the end the measures pass and we improve safety.

Not so with gun control. The laws about guns are puny, watered down and ineffective. You can buy ammo through the Internet in quantities that raise no alarm. The gun vendor does not think about the motive of his customer or the consequences of his sale. What would a 20-year-old want with a rapid-fire gun? The gun vendor acts as if it is none of his business to inquire. He can wash his hands off and call it a deal the minute the gun buyer leaves his store.

As to deliberate non-accidental deaths by cars, they are hard to quantify outside of recent terror attacks. People just don't regard cars as weapons. Guns are the preferred weapon of choice, especially for homicides. They do use cars for suicide sometimes. Sometimes they drive off a cliff or they crash against something at 90 miles per hour. But this is iffy and does not always ensure death. The most common way of using a car to commit suicide is by revving up the engine in a closed garage and dying from carbon monoxide poisoning.

The More Guns, the Better

In 1982 the town of Kennesaw, Georgia, passed an ordinance requiring its citizens to keep guns in their homes. This was done to pique the town of Morton Grove, Illinois, which had passed legislation banning guns. Over the years the comfort level and the appetite for guns have increased to such a point that now more and more state legislatures are passing bills allowing people to have guns not only in their homes, but in school areas, in churches and now even in college campuses.

The idea that more guns are better is absurd, counter-intuitive, and at variance with the facts. Can they not see that we have more guns than any civilized country in the world and are paying the price by having the highest number of gun deaths year after year? We are forcing water down the throat of a man half-drowned.

The only beneficiaries of this wacky idea are the NRA, the gun manufacturers, the gun dealers, and the politicians who are paid handsomely for their vote. The hype for more and more guns distorts our values and warps our common sense. Guns are elevated to a lofty level they do not merit when they are touted as guarantors of self-defense, as useful, or as necessary tools of survival. Self-defense and deterrence are undelivered promises; they are goals that guns have failed to achieve so far. They are more like excuses for an addiction, like a gambler who is deeply in debt and deludes himself into thinking that the next bet is the winner. We are arming ourselves beyond all reason for the illusory payoff of safety through more guns. The people who believe this have turned reality upside down. They are not looking at facts. They are chasing a myth.

In the Gadarene rush to flood the land with more guns, we are invading gun-free sanctuaries such as churches and college campuses. The state legislators are all too eager to pursue it for purely selfish reasons. They do so even when they face opposition to their scheme from the people who would be most affected by it. In the case of college campuses, virtually everyone from the regents down to the administrators, the professors and the students object to it; they don't want the guns on campus. The legislators push ahead despite their objections, cramming it down their throats. Their motivation is not only selfish, but it reeks of hypocrisy. They want guns on the college campuses, but they don't want them on their turf, in the state capitols.

How can people persist in clamoring for more guns and insist on introducing them into areas that have been heretofore safe havens? We are already the most heavily armed among civilized countries. There are already more than 300 million guns in the U.S. out of a population of roughly 320 million. That is almost a gun for every man, woman and child. Actually, only about a third of all Americans own a firearm. Second, the gun death rate for the U.S. is the highest among comparable civilized nations. Here is a brief recap for year 2010.

	GUNS per 100	GUN DEATHS
United States	88.0	32,163
France	31.2	1,736
Germany	30.3	819
Canada	30.8	781
U.K.	6.2	145
Australia	15.0	232

Source: "Gun Ownership and Firearm-related Deaths," by Drs. Sripal Bangalore and Franz H. Messerli, *The American Journal of Medicine*, October 2013, Volume 126, pp. 873-876.

And yet, we want more. I simply cannot picture having more guns in more places as any panacea to gun violence. I find it easier to picture just the opposite. I do not believe that criminals will be daunted by the knowledge that every man, woman and child is armed. The criminals would know that many of the other gun wielders are wimps and meek lambs, who may own the guns, but are not killers and lack the cold blood to win in a gun confrontation. Criminals would always have the element of surprise and would be hardened to use their guns. In no time we would have a Wild West redux where the game became survival of the quickest, and the meanest. We would reach a point in which the state would tell people: every man for himself! Arm yourselves! Become warriors! Fight for your life! You are on your own. The state cannot defend you.

How can anyone think that living in such a brutish, dog-eat-dog world could be peaceful? The shootings would turn more and more cities into Chicago-like war zones full of gang violence and vendettas. The meek and kind would be slaughtered because they wouldn't have the cold blood and savagery to survive. When the shooting started and they were caught in the cross fire, they wouldn't even know who was bad, who was good; they would run for cover and try to get out of that melee. The country would be in a virtual state of war, as some streets of Chicago are even now.

People fail to understand the dynamics of the gun. They think the gun confers deterrence and protection and fail to consider other effects. The gun also imparts uncertainty, fear, distrust, paranoia and misunderstanding, which often lead to fatal miscalculations. In many instances police reaction is triggered by the charged atmosphere of gun threats, more so than racism. Police blunders are so rampant and so lethal that they deserve especial treatment. I deal with this in Chapter 15, Police and Guns. We are beginning to learn our lessons as we continue social experimentation with guns.

Some states have ventured into "open carry" mode. People can carry their guns in full display. The assumption is that informing others that you are armed would deter untoward action towards you. Your gun is serving notice to the world. You are not bluffing. Colorado is one such open carry state.

But an incident occurred in Colorado Springs on October 31, 2015 which made people wonder whether the open-carry business is a good idea. They discovered an unintended consequence of "open carry." It helps a killer by affording him precious time to ready himself so he can commit murder unimpeded. He can stand on his front yard, readying his gun and setting himself up. There is no point in calling the police because he is not doing anything illegal. If you called the police, they would not respond because he has not broken any law. It is only when he starts shooting and killing people that you can report him. But by then it is too late.

A man did just that in Colorado Springs. After fully loading and setting himself up in his front yard, he started shooting at passersby, managing to kill a young fellow on a bike and two other women walking by. http://www.cnn.com/2015/10/31/us/colorado-springs-shooting/.

The idea that we can achieve peace by giving both predator and prey a gun is too facile. It ignores other realities that will never equalize the playing field. The predator will have the will, the expertise and cold blood to use the gun. And that is a significant advantage.

A better solution is to have neither predator nor prey armed with guns. If peace and safety is what we want, then it is much better to go towards a world free of guns. It is not hard to picture such a world because it already exists right here in the U.S. Just go to a major airport and see hundreds of people walking worry free, feeling safe because they are unthreatened by the gun. Airports are the only places in America where the Second Amendment is trumped without debate or arguments. You are frisked and you are X-rayed. If you are armed, you are disarmed on the spot. No ifs, no buts.

Or, consider another situation: a hell hole full of evil men, all rotten murderers with a lust to kill –but unarmed. This is a penitentiary where only the guards have arms. Here we have the will to kill, but not the guns with which to do it. I will be the first to allow that killing is not totally eradicated here. The killers do manage to choke and stab. But the lethality is considerably reduced.

AN ARMED CITIZENRY PREVENTS GOVERNMENT TYRANNY

Some gun lovers are driven by paranoia and deliriums of invincibility. They distrust government and they are deluded enough to believe that the U.S. Government would be tyrannical were it not for the guns that the citizenry possesses. So, they need to stay armed and get even more guns. This people fancy themselves as the "well armed militia" of the Second Amendment. They want to be ready for the day when the government troops (the posse comitatus) comes after them.

It is difficult to tell whether these people really believe they could stand against the might of the United States armed forces, or whether it is just bravado, or whether they just love fantasizing about the fight.

Tyranny is not new, especially in other parts of the world and in the past. But we are talking about the United States here. For America, in this day and age, militaristic tyranny against its citizens is far-fetched. But defenders of their paranoia like to offer these historical events, and not always accurately, as examples of what they are talking about.

Massacre at Wounded Knee (1890)
The Posse Comitatus Act (1878)
The Wounded Knee Incident (1973)
The Camp Davidian Stand-off at Waco (1993)
The Nazis' gun confiscation policies (pre-WWII)

Some of these were confrontations which went awry, protests that escalated to violence from misunderstandings. Shots were fired and war broke out. This is the case for the Wounded Knee and the Waco incidents.

Some people misunderstand what Posse Comitatus means and think it is empowerment of the citizens against the government. Actually, this is an act which Congress passed during the Reconstruction, ten years after the Civil War, to limit the powers of the federal government in using federal military personnel to enforce state laws. By this act, the President removed federal troops from Southern states.

But *The Enforcement Acts* provide exception to the Posse Comitatus law. President Eisenhower used the power in these acts to send federal troops into Little Rock in 1958. At that time the President had no other recourse but to call up military forces, because the State of Arkansas would not protect the safety and Constitutional rights of some of its people.

As to the Nazi situation in Germany, they need to get real. Do the gun advocates believe that the German citizens armed with only Lugers and pistols stood a chance against one of the most powerful military machines of the world in the 1930s and '40s? Neither Poland, Czechoslovakia, Holland, nor France with all their armies, or with their air force could stop him. It took great, great effort for England, Russia and the United States to defeat Nazi Germany.

The only way to stop a massacre is ...

The only way to stop a massacre is to have a good guy with a gun kill a bad guy with a gun. How very convenient for the seller of guns to suggest this. La Pierre himself, the head of the NRA, came up with this.

It is human to fantasize in the aftermath of a tragedy, rewinding time to cheat fate out of what it has already written into history. What if the killer's gun had malfunctioned? What if he had had an accident on the way to the massacre? What if Superman, or Batman, or any of our mythical cartoon heroes had materialized in the nick of time and killed the gunman? What if one of the victims, one of the good guys, had had a gun?

We all fantasize. The difference is that most of us snap out of these wistful hallucinations, but La Pierre holds on to his fantasy and, unfortunately, he is in a position to foist this fantasy as viable gun policy.

Who is the good guy that La Pierre is thinking about? Is it a kindergarten teacher? What weapons would she be armed with? Could she, with her wimpy revolver, stop a war veteran who has gone rogue and is armed with an AK-47? Even police departments across the land complain that they are under-gunned when they face highly armed criminals. Or should we train our teachers to be Marines and arm them to the hilt? This is a recipe for an arms race, a weapons escalation. Is this what we want? Is there no other alternative?

A better way to stop a massacre is by preventing the bad guy from getting a gun in the first place, or, if he got one, by keeping him from using it. Here is how.

* Before we pass more laws, let us begin by enforcing the laws we already have. Right now buying guns is as easy as buying groceries. The bad guys don't need to steal the guns and they don't need black markets either. They can just go to a so-called "bad apple" gun shop near them. According to a CNN report, (https://rubengallego.house.gov/media-center/in-the-news/crack-down-bad-apple-gun-dealers) it is estimated that 5% of these bad apple stores are involved in 90% of the guns involved in crimes.

We cannot put our trust on the gun stores. Their motivation is profit from gun sales, not fighting crime. If a gun dealer suspected that a buyer was a murderer or was a front for a straw sale, he has no incentive to act on his suspicion. That would just complicate his business. He need not go beyond the law to aid society. His concern is the superficial one of crossing the t's and dotting the i's so that when the killing does take place, he could say he did everything by the book.

* Many bad apple stores wouldn't even bother with crossing the t's. They don't need to because they can count on the laxity of law enforcement. Cops have better things to do. The ATF (Alcohol, Tobacco and Firearms) is understaffed and under-budgeted.

* The office of the Attorney General of the US could and should do something about this, but it won't. It's a hot potato politically. It would take a very committed president with strong congressional support to undertake this. Even then, a long drawn and acrimonious fight could be expected. At present we are not ready for that.

While the cash registers keep clicking with gun sales to both good guys and bad guys, it is the bad guys who keep doing the killing. One hardly ever hears of the good guy with gun saving the day. Remarkably, the gun research organization *Everytown* makes this significant statement in this regard:

There is not a single mass shooting in Everytown's database in which the shooter was stopped by an armed civilian —even in cases where there were armed civilians present. See: "Most Mass Shootings Do Not Occur in Gun-free zones," **HTTPS://EVERYTOWNRESEARCH.ORG/REPORTS/ MASS-SHOOTINGS-ANALYSIS/?NCID=EDLINKUSHPMG00000313**

Incredibly, in the instances when the shooter has been stopped, the good guys were unarmed. Two recent cases come to mind.

On August 21, 2015 three Americans —Alek Skarlatos, Spencer Stone and Anthony Sadler —overpowered a Moroccan national armed with an

AK gun on a high speed train bound for Paris. The three American were decorated by the French Prime Minister for their heroic intervention.

On October 1, 2015 a shooting took place at the Umpqua Community College, near Roseburg, Oregon. Nine persons were killed by Christopher Harper-Mercer. Chris Mintz blocked a door with his body to allow his class to escape. He next left the building to alert students in the library to evacuate. Returning to the shooting scene, he advised a wounded student to stay down and be quiet. At that point Mercer leaned out from the classroom into the hallway and shot Mintz five times. But Mintz survived.

In this same incident there were several students armed with handguns who did not intervene in order to avoid confusing the law enforcement officers on the scene. I quote *Everytown* again.

"As one student, a military veteran who was carrying a concealed gun at the time, explained: 'Luckily, we made the choice not to get involved…not knowing where SWAT was on their response time, they wouldn't know who we were, and if we had our guns ready to shoot, they'd think we were the bad guys.'" **HTTPS://EVERYTOWNRESEARCH. ORG/REPORTS/MASS-SHOOTINGS-ANALYSIS/?NCID= EDLINKUSHPMG00000313**

This shows that La Pierre's whimsy about a good guy with a gun stopping a bad guy with a gun is downright impractical. It is not that easy and it is extremely dangerous. The devil is always in the details and the details in this case are numerous and insuperable.

GUNS ARE CRUEL, THE ELECTRIC CHAIR IS NOT

Let it not be said that I am totally against the use of guns for killing people. In fact, at times I highly recommend it and I decry –I repeat decry –that we are not allowed to use guns in executions. The idiocy in this instance does not derive from the gun lovers –for once I am on their side. The idiocy is with the government or whoever it was that banned the firing squad in death penalty executions.

It is curious and incomprehensible to me that for all the perfervid love that Americans have for guns, guns are not used in carrying out the death penalty. Instead we choose lethal injection and the electric chair, which are bizarre, grotesque and macabre forms of execution. They are also most ineffective because something does go awry more often than one could imagine, resulting in horrid torture for everyone concerned. Lately, it has become an opera buffa. Some have charged that these forms of execution are cruel and unusual punishment. There are delays in some executions because pharmacies cannot find the chemicals or are refusing to supply them. Then there is also disagreement and debate about the right mix of chemicals. Why do we complicate things so stupidly?

By contrast, bullets are cheap and they have proven their efficacy most unfailingly. Also, there is no dearth of volunteers to carry out the execution. As I recall, in Utah, the last state to use firing squads (in the execution of Gary Gilmore, 1977), they always had more avid volunteers for the death squad than were needed. Volunteers had to be turned away, which does not surprise me.

I ask the NRA, since they have a way with guns and with Congress, that they see to it that all executions be by firing squad.

CHAPTER 6

On the Innocence of Guns

● ● ●

THE MANTRA THAT GUNS DON'T kill people and only people kill people is based on the notion that guns are inanimate objects; that they are brainless non-living things and that they have no mobility or will of their own. They carry no grudges; they are incapable of hating, incapable of scheming, of transporting themselves, of loading themselves and of aiming and shooting. Therefore, they are innocent. Only humans have volition; only humans can feel and carry grudges; only humans have the wherewithal to carry out malice. Therefore, humans and only humans are the culprits. Guns should be fully absolved of all blame and should be left alone. Don't even think of curtailing or punishing such innocent creatures. It would be a grievous miscarriage of justice.

This argument is just a ruse, a rebuttal to an imaginary claim that nobody ever made. It is a made-up issue. Nobody claims that guns have will of their own, or that they can load themselves. The real issue is the inseparable and inextricable involvement between man and gun in a killing. Gun advocates attempt to separate this involvement and then attempt magic to make the gun disappear. But their amateurish trick fails; it lacks legerdemain and savoir faire. Everyone can still see the gun after the abracadabra.

Most people have no trouble seeing that once a gun comes under man's control it becomes as one with him. Man and gun become inseparable. The gun is an extension of man's body, a minion of man's will.

And man, in turn, is made powerful by the gun, with the omnipotence of life and death over others. It is only when guns are stored and locked up in an armory that they are as dumb as rocks.

No one in his right mind would question the synchronicity, the singularity of purpose that man and gun can forge when they come together. Man avails himself of the gun's killing efficiency, and the gun, in turn, draws on the malevolence and madness of its master creating a vortex of reciprocal accommodation. The man's finger coils around the trigger as if it were just another bone of his hand. There is no distance between metal and skin. Physical resistance is so minimal that even a child can fire the gun. From the man's brain flow the nerve charges that travel through his pleural nexus all the way to the finger coiled around the trigger which is flirting to be squeezed, eager to vomit the barrage of bullets in its gut. Why deny this consummation of purpose and complicity? It's like claiming that killings occur by Immaculate Misconception.

The role of the gun is not thinking, or scheming, or planning, or stalking and setting traps or carrying grudges, or making decisions. The man does that for them. The role of the gun is to be available, to be reliable and efficient; to not jam or misfire; to spew out bullets at the stipulated rate with unbiased aim and to fulfill the destructive reason for which it was created. The guilt of the gun derives not from what the gun is willing to do, but from what it is capable of doing when under the control of man. Over the years guns have become more deadly and accommodating. We have come a long way since the klutzy muskets of centuries ago.

But gun lovers are obsessed about decriminalizing the gun. They warp reality to the limit to turn guns into innocent artifacts, into necessary household implements. So, they come up with this ruse that since guns have no volition of their own, they cannot kill. For years they have foisted this canard on the American people, sending us on a chase after the man but not the gun. "The killer went that a way," they tell us, while they guard and protect the other culprit, the gun. That is how the gun has won its liberty to kill again and again and continues to have a free pass in America through the carnage of 33,000 gun deaths per year, which is the highest in the world among civilized nations.

The coordination for a kill between man and gun begins with a long period of apprenticeship. You just don't pick up a gun seconds before a shooting and try to familiarize yourself with its functioning. You don't pick up a gun and go to your kill assuming that the gun is loaded. You make sure that it is. You also make sure that it is working. You make sure that you know how to handle it, how to aim it, how to fire it and reload it. To avoid hassles, you hide it as you carry it to your killing rendezvous. In sum, you work in sundry ways at your nefarious task. Gun lovers engage in these tasks; they do them all the time and they love it. They are devoted to their gun; they pamper it; they clean it; they oil it; and they shoot it in dry runs.

It is odd, therefore, that after all this preparation, after all this togetherness and teamwork; after all the apprenticeship, the rehearsals and dry runs, that anyone should try to disavow this friendship and partnership and betray the gun by not giving it credit for its part, weaseling out on the weapon that did so much for the shooter. The gun that did not jam, that did not malfunction, that fired on cue is robbed of its credit. Such naked ingratitude from gun users should be punishable by firing squad...if only the guns could avenge their betrayal.

Measures of Guilt. Man and gun share guilt, but not always equally. Circumstances can change the level of guilt involved. There are situations where the greater share of the guilt belongs to the man. And there are other situations where the gun makes a virtual clean sweep of the guilt.

How would you rate the guilt in this situation? A gun obeys the shooter on the first two kills, but jams after that, saving ten others who would have been easily killed like fish in a barrel. It is as if victims' prayers had been heard and answered, thwarting the man who would have gone on killing. It is as if the gun responded to the pleas of the would-be victims and not at the commands of its master. In fairness, therefore, we must acknowledge the gun's auspicious role and recognize that its guilt is lower than that of the shooter. The gun deserves our gratitude here.

Or, it could happen that an ostensibly innocent weapon such as a toy gun, a facsimile of a weapon that cannot fire, that cannot kill, is not as innocent as it appears on first blush. A toy gun can manage to invite firepower, causing death to its wielder.

Or, who could imagine that at times a gun can be guiltier than the shooter himself? This happens when there is no malicious intent, when the shooter doesn't even know what a gun is, as when a two-year-old child gets hold of a gun and fires it, killing someone. This is a killing, but it is not a homicide. The law rules in favor of the human.

Then we come to the cases when the gun has a satanic power and becomes a human manipulator. Here guilt gushes forth in an avalanche of wickedness that takes possession of the worst instincts of man. The gun senses his rage and manipulates the man, turning him into a puppet, into the gun's rag doll.

Finally, we have something uniquely American: the collective guilt for the mess that the gun has gotten us into. This involves us all. We cannot cop out saying: "I wasn't there; I didn't pull the trigger; I don't even own a gun and never have." All that may be true, but the guilt and blame still touches all of us because we are in this together, caught in a swamp of guns, snarled by our laws such as they are, and stuck in the political morass that makes it all happen. As long as this continues, we all share in the guilt –whether we own a gun or not. The NRA swaddles us all with guilt.

Now let us amplify on the various situations of man and gun guilt introduced above.

The Ideal Gun. If there were such a thing, where would one find it? What would be its attributes? Such a gun, if it existed, could only be found in fantasy land. The smart gun has some of its desirable characteristics because it fools a criminal into thinking he can fire it, but the gun refuses as it is programmed to obey a designated person only. Some of the other mythical characteristics of the ideal gun would be the antithesis of the real ones. The guns would be big, heavy, unwieldy, awkward and klutzy. They would also be temperamental and unreliable, difficult to load and fire. They would have a high learning curve that required a long period of apprenticeship. Such guns would be inept accessories that would enhance the chance of botched killing attempts. They would serve society so well that we would be obliged to confer upon them badges and medals. Imagine what an ideal situation it would be to live in a society where only the police had the real AR-15s while all guns available to criminals were the unwieldy klutzy ones.

Being difficult to operate, requiring extensive training and experience and malfunctioning often, they would foil killings and trap perps. Hallelujah! Such guns would lure fools into using them, only to thwart them and get them caught. It would be almost as if the guns tripped up the killers on purpose. The guns' misfiring and their jamming would lower the death rate while at the same time raising the apprehension rate for failed murderers. What could be better? This is such a win-win scenario that it is tempting to rig the real guns so as to bring it about.

How far we are from such a world! This mythical gun helps us realize the gravity of our disarray. Our urban settings are populated with guns of military prowess available to anyone. The guns in the hands of criminals are not heavy but ultralight, easy to fire and they can spew out bullets with blitzkrieg speed and mow down people with deadly efficiency, turning our malls and urban idylls into killing fields. The hierarchy of firepower is all wrong. We have conferred too much firepower on ordinary people, corrupting them out of their sanity. Meanwhile the police and the military which are meant to be our lines of defense often encounter criminals that are better armed. We must reverse this imbalance even if we have to redesign the guns and change the laws so as to reduce the killing potential of ordinary citizens and keep the monster weapons in the hands of authorities. We must reduce the number of monster guns that can fire at the rate of 45 bullets per minute with over-kill to spare and which now roam freely everywhere. We must ban these guns from our sanctuaries, from our homes, from our college campuses and our churches. They do not belong in people's homes. It is inconceivable that someone would want to defend these monsters as blameless, given the carnage they cause. Only the NRA.

The toy gun. On first blush, one would think that the safest, the least harmful and ostensibly the most innocent gun, is a toy gun. But we are fooled by appearances. The toy gun also has a sinister dimension that can make it deadly.

Although the toy gun cannot fire bullets, it has the ability to draw fire upon its wielder by the fear it imparts on one who does not know it is a toy, one who feels threatened by it and who happens to have a real gun. The threatened individual can react to the toy's threat with real firepower. In the inflammable world we live in, where the air we breathe is suffused with the threat and peril of the gun, the call to shoot waits for no spark. It bursts on its own with a barrage of bullets from the spontaneity of fear.

The number of cases where kids in the US have gotten killed because they brandished a toy gun is more than one can digest without choking! Usually, it occurs at the hands of the police, and this strange denouement opens up another disgusting can of worms. Here are four cases that made the news within the last four years. All the victims were teenagers.

Robert Dentmond, a 16-year old in Gainesville, Fl was killed when brandishing a gun. According to some reports he wanted to commit suicide. The police accommodated him with a barrage of bullets. Source: Rob C Witzel, *The Gainesville Sun*, March 21, 2016.

Tyree King, a 13-year old in Columbus, OH was wielding a BB gun when he was shot by police. Source: *MSNBC*, September 16, 2016.

Andy Lopez, a 13-year old in Santa Rosa, CA was carrying a pellet gun that looked like an assault rifle when he was killed by sheriff's deputies. Source: Robin Wilkey, *Huffpost*, October 23, 2013.

Tamir Rice, a 12-year old in Cleveland, OH was armed with a pellet gun on a city recreation center when he was shot by police. Source: *CBCV News*, November 23, 2014.

There is extensive information on the trials and sequels of these cases. You can Google the cases and learn what happened to the policemen on duty, how much remuneration the victim's family got and more. But on the face of things, it appears to me that the policemen on the beat need more training to better handle these situations and more restraint. Granting that not knowing that they are dealing with a toy gun rushes the adrenalin. But the inescapable fact is that in the end the police were the *first and only* shooters in these cases. And this is quite an indictment.

These situations call for a measured graduated response that should allow time to do its work and answer questions that define the situation for what it is. The longer the potential shooter fails to fire his gun, the higher the probability that his gun is not lethal. Add the fact that if he is a kid, then there is a good chance that his gun is a toy since he could not have bought a real one; or if he borrowed or stole one, he may not even know how to fire it. But instead of patience to ascertain the nature of the situation, we get no warning shots, no shots aimed to maim. We get a barrage of bullets with irreversible deadly consequences. This is patently wrong.

The wayward gun. Here the shooter is innocent, but the gun, by all counts, seems guiltier. In these cases there is no complicity, no malevolent human intent. And yet, the gun fulfilled its destiny and killed practically on its own. Sadly, these occurrences are very, very real – nothing mythical about them.

For example, a gun was left unattended or unsecured and a child got hold of it and without intent or premeditation the gun went BANG! The child managed to kill a sibling, not knowing what he was doing, not knowing that guns can kill, not knowing what death is. Or the gun owner is careless and does not realize the gun is loaded, but it is. Or in a hunt you shoot at another hunter, thinking it was a deer. Or in a melee, you hit an innocent bystander. Or you drop the gun accidentally and it goes off. Guns are so on the edge of calamity that it doesn't take much for them to take a life of their own. Human stupidity, carelessness and recklessness are like long spectral fingers that wrap around the gun's trigger to produce death and tragedy even when there is no killing intent, even when the gun owner is elsewhere.

The controlling gun. This is the most dangerous and harmful property of the gun. It emerges when the gun is in possession of an aggressor, of an abuser, of a man who has rage in his blood. The gun seems to recognize this and has the insidious power to take advantage of the man and the situation. This psychological role of the gun, this ability to influence man, to change him and to direct his actions is the most potent form of gun guilt. Some men cannot countervail this power of the gun. Guns imbue them with a sense of omnipotence that makes them feel like avenging gods. When they are under this spell, anything can set them off: a scorn, a rebuff, an insult, a bad gesture. It is then that guns can become human manipulators. They give the offended man the power to settle scores on the spot and mete out justice with bullets. Road rage turns into murder. The gun becomes the murderous little devil that rides on the shoulder of the gun packer whispering: Kill! Kill! Kill! This voice is so strong that at some point the gun becomes the puppeteer and man the mere ragdoll. That is why it is appalling to contemplate the proposals by state legislatures across the country to inundate the land with more guns and force them into such gun-free sanctuaries as airports and college campuses. They don't even think about the potential monsters they are giving guns to.

I will revisit this satanic power of the gun in the next two chapters where I consider the conditional probability of aggression given a gun.

Collective guilt. The guilt for the gun deaths in this country extends beyond the shooter and the gun. Our legislators and the NRA should share in the guilt. Although they were not present at the killing sites and did not pull the trigger themselves, they are responsible because they have saturated the country with guns and have created the conditions that make many gun deaths inevitable. To a lesser extent the police should share some of the guilt as well. Their training, their protocol and their equipment is inadequate for the dangerous situations they are forced to confront. Finally, all of us are splattered with gun blood because we don't do enough to change our laws, to change our attitudes about guns, to change the scales that favor gun rights over safety and to change the indifference to so much bloodshed on account of guns.

CHAPTER 7

Guns, Aggression and Conditional Probabilities

● ● ●

PROBABILITIES ARE NOT USER FRIENDLY. Over many years of teaching the subject, I know how difficult they can be. But sometimes, given a good intuitive example, they can come alive and become virtually tangible even to those who are a little allergic to them. So bear with me.

Let's begin intuitively, considering the differences between a convent full of nuns and a prison full of murderers. What's the difference? Why don't we allow guns in prisons? And what would happen if we armed the convent?

A penitentiary full of murderers has the combustible atmosphere of spilled gasoline. Adding guns would be like throwing a lit match into it. This metaphor vivifies the conditional probability that someone will attack given that he has a gun, $P(A/G)$. In all, we need three probabilities. They are:

$P(G)$ the probability the person is armed with a gun.
$P(A/G)$ the probability he will attack, given that he has a gun.
$P(AG)$ the probability he does attack with a gun

There is a very useful equation, known as the Multiplication Rule, which shows how these probabilities are connected:

7.1 $P(AG) = P(G) \, P(A/G)$

The probability on the left-side –that a gun-attack will actually take place –is the one of ultimate interest, the one we will be pursuing in the ensuing discussions.

Common sense and the multiplication rule above both confirm this bit of wisdom. If there are no guns in prison, then P(G)=0 and there can be no gun attacks. The multiplication rule puts this statement this way:

$$P(AG) = (0) \times P(A/G) = 0.$$

So, regardless of the explosiveness of the conditional probability P(A/G), the prison is safe because there are no guns. The same holds in the convents, since they also have no guns. So far this is all very true but trivial. The absence of guns frustrates the killings. Let's make it more challenging. What would happen if we introduced 80 guns in both places? Now P(A/G) comes into play.

Convent

	G	G'	Totals
A	0	0	0
A'	80	20	100
Totals	80	20	100

Prison

	G	G'	Totals
A	78	16	94
A'	2	4	6
Totals	80	20	100

The populations of convent and prison are both 100. There the similarities end. The convent exudes virtue, kindness, devotion, peacefulness and love of God. The nuns have renounced so much of the world by taking vows of silence, of chastity, of poverty. The above table reflects this. There isn't a single nun who would attack anyone with any weapon, (gun or other), and, accordingly, the row for attacks of any sort is zero in the convent. All the nuns are on the row A' which represent non-attackers; 80 of them have guns, which they do not fire; and 20 of them have no guns.

By contrast, the majority of the inmates are attackers. There are 94 aggressors and 6 non aggressors. Of the 80 guns in the inmates' possession, 78 are used to attack others and two are kept idle. There are 20 inmates without guns; of these, 16 attacked others with weapons other than guns. Only 4 of the unarmed inmates attacked no one. With these figures in hand it is possible to calculate the conditional probabilities for the convent and the prison, thus:

Convent: $P(A/G) = 0/80 = 0$ Prison: $P(A/G) = 78/80 = 0.975$

Here is where we find the critical difference between the two institutions. The convent imparts a peaceful and serene quality because its conditional probability $P(A/G)$ is zero. It has the smell of roses, the sound of peace. In addition, because $P(A)$ also happens to be zero in the convent, the events A and G (aggression and guns) are said to be *independent*. This means that the likelihood of aggression in the convent is unaffected by guns. To see this intuitively, note that without guns the probability of aggression is $P(A) = 0$. But with guns, the probability of aggression is still $P(A/G) = 0$. Therefore, introducing the guns changed nothing. The events are independent.

The prison is entirely different. The proclivity for aggression is $P(A/G) = 78/80 = 0.975$, which is very high. This is what saturates the prison air with impending danger. It is the mathematical embodiment of the prison's charged atmosphere. Moreover, in the prison case A and G are *dependent* events, meaning that guns do change things by exacerbating the danger. To see this note that without guns the probability that an inmate will attack is $P(A) = 0.94$. But if he has a gun, the probability he will attack rises to $P(A/G) = 78/80 = 0.975$. Hence, a gun raises the probability of aggression in the prison. The events are dependent.

We now have the wherewithal to calculate $P(AG)$, the aggression by guns, and to carry out a comparison of the violence in the two places. We invoke the Multiplication Rule, giving us:

Convent: $P(AG) = P(G)P(A/G) = 0.80 \times 0 = 0$.

Behold! There are no gun-attacks in the convent despite the fact that there are 80 guns among the nuns now. The zero-value of the convent's conditional probability completely mollifies the killing potential of the guns. No gun attacks materialize.

At the prison it is a different story. The proclivity for aggression is 0.975, a value so high that it is red hot with malice. It throbs. It seethes. Invoking the multiplication rule we see its effect:

Prison: $P(AG) = P(G)P(A/G) = 0.80 \times 0.975 = 0.78$

In order to make this expression more intuitive, let me multiply both sides by 100 and re-express it in this equivalent way:

$$100P(AG) = 80 \times 0.975 = 78$$

This reads: the expected number of gun attacks, 78, is virtually equal to the number of guns introduced, meaning that gun attacks rise almost one-to-one with the guns. Out of the 80 guns introduced into the prison only two are not used to attack anyone. Guns are very busy in prison. They don't just sit idle as they do in the convent, they are fired to kill.

The above figures are hypothetical and are intended to clarify the nature of conditional probabilities in scenarios where safety and danger are indisputably manifest. It is possible that the gun attacks could have been a little lower, say 70 instead of 78. Or they could have been a little higher, say 80. We will never know the real values because this is an experiment that cannot be carried out. We cannot –and should not –introduce guns into the convent or the prison to find out. But the conceptual experiment helps us envision the role of $P(A/G)$, which is palpable and intelligible in these examples.

Summarizing, $P(A/G)$ is the factor that, depending on its value, either feeds gun violence or quells it. It is explosive in the prison. It is unthreatening, calming as fresh snow in the convent. Also, if you have two communities or two individuals, one with a low $P(A/G)$ and the other with a high $P(A/G)$, and you give them guns, the one with the higher $P(A/G)$ will have more gun violence. This is axiomatic. The multiplication rule above confirms it unequivocally. This, after all, is why we don't allow guns in prisons.

The experiment also raises other intriguing and tantalizing questions. According to some, introducing more guns is always a good thing. Supposedly it deters potential trouble makers when they know others are armed. But could this apply in prison? Are potential attackers deterred when they know their victims are armed? Could the gun saturation in the prison turn into a cold war where the guns are idle for fear of Armageddon? Or would the proliferation of guns in a prison lead to purges and blood baths?

I don't believe in the détente scenario. I believe a blood bath will ensue whether it is bad guys killing good guys or vice versa. I believe the idea of being armed as a way of daunting others and thus enhancing your self-protection does not work in a dog-eat-dog world. A prison full of murderers is like the ghettos of Chicago, where a perverse dynamic is engendered by the combination of evil and guns. Killings explode exponentially and self-defense is corrupted, morphing into something akin to revenge rationalized as belated self-defense, or aggression justified as pre-emptive self-defense.

Normally, true self-defense is characterized by a lagged reaction to some threat. The potential victim is first alerted by a signal from the aggressor. The signal could be an actual act of aggression that missed or misfired; or it could be a provocative movement, a prelude to the real thing, a turn, a reaching, or a posturing that precipitated self-defense in the nick of time. The lag from threat to reaction may be short, but there is a lag. Not so in communities and situations such as the above where practically everyone is armed and where shootings are rampant. In such conditions the inflammable atmosphere precludes prudence. You are reacting to history, to a way of life, to aggression in the air and you have to be faster than the next guy. This is the Wild West and here a new motto evolves: "You die first, brother. I can't sit around and wait for you to shoot first. Self-defense means I shoot first, before you even think of messing with me." So, eventually self-defense becomes pre-emptive aggression and is justified as a cardinal rule of survival in the jungle.

CHAPTER 8

Guns, Domestic Violence and Mass Shootings

● ● ●

AGGRESSION IS AN INHERENT TRAIT that some men carry for years, some-times going back to elementary school days when they were little bul-lies already. But, unless there are official complaints and police records, an aggressor's history is his dirty little secret. If by chance he is discov-ered, he can move to another place and start with a clean slate. There is no indelible letter "A" etched to his forehead to permanently brand him. There are no x-rays, no urine or blood tests to confirm his hidden potential danger. Background checks will detect nothing. Therefore, it is not possible to apply the probability analysis of the previous chapter to him.

Unarmed, an aggressor is non-lethal, a monster with undeveloped fangs. But once he gets a gun, he is a ticking time bomb, a danger to friends, to relatives and to himself. Anything can set him off. If he is jilted, scorned, or fired from a job, the gun is his justice maker. At the first provocation he is apt to spring out like a jack-in-the-box and attack. His victim could be a young spouse who suddenly discovers that she married a monster; or it could be the cop who rushes to her rescue and comes face to face with his rage and his bullet; or it could be a driver who discovers that he made the mistake of his life when he cut off the aggressor on traffic and triggered his road rage.

Only those who are close to the aggressor and who have seen his rage are wise to his dark side. But their information is often insubstan-tial, as it is a chronicle of blowups, like the time he killed a family pet, or the time he threatened vaguely (half in gest) to kill someone, or the time he broke grandma's china wantonly. In the eyes of the law these tantrums are just hearsay and carry no weight in background checks, which is as it should be.

There is little we can do to prevent aggressors who have no police records from getting guns. This is a vulnerability for which there is no protection and it should give us pause when we consider how many people the NRA invites and urges to get guns. Some of those gun purchasers will pass the background checks with flying colors but could be closet aggressors. For this reason, we should do everything in our power to slow down the sale of guns and encourage people to wait, to reflect and become better informed before rushing to buy guns. Unfortunately, the NRA and some state legislatures are doing just the opposite. They are opening the flood gates of guns for the masses, and allowing guns in more and more places, reducing our gun-free sanctuaries such as airports, churches and college campuses. The zeal to sell guns is driven by the delusion that every American needs a gun and every potential buyer is a docile responsible individual who will not use his gun to kill.

But what if the individual is not a closet aggressor but an out-and-out aggressor, a man who has a record of violence and abuse? Can we predict that he will commit gun violence? Of course we can. Although we may not be able to put a specific number on the probability, we know his $P(A/G)$ is very high and is as flammable as a blanket soaked in gasoline. He is dangerous. The question is not whether he will attack, but when. This man should not have access to a gun. He should be kept away from his potential victims. But, sadly, we fail at this.

We are inept at controlling the gun violence even when we are dealing with a ticking time bomb. For a dozen reasons this aggressor will slip through our fingers and commit mass murder. We have so many loops and crannies that he is able to consummate his massacre unimpeded. This happens many times in this country, much too often. Here are the particulars.

Sometimes, we know the man is an aggressor; he has been branded as such by the police and the courts. Everyone knows him to be a cad, a heel, a violent and cruel ogre in the community. He is a domestic abuser. The police have had runs with him and judges have passed restraining orders on him. His rap sheet is so long and bloody that it would make Satan proud. Anybody would tell you that this man is a walking volcano and that the probability he would go on a killing rampage is a virtual certainty.

And yet, it is mind boggling and inexcusable that despite the warnings, despite the anticipation, this man manages to get the guns, the ammo and the wherewithal to carry out his massacre. It would be bad enough if this was a rare, once-every-quarter-century occurrence. But it happens in America every year again and again. It has become our brand of tragedy, with its special American imprint that could be labeled the recurring fulfillment of massacres foretold. Why does it recur so frequently? Is it that we don't care? Or are we so dumb that we never learn from experience? How could we fail to prevent killings which are so predictable? Why do we fail to protect people from these monsters? Here are some of the specifics.

* We focus too much on gun purchases as opposed to gun possession. For example, the laws in some states ban the aggressor from buying a gun. But if he already has one, the law has no provision to requisition the gun. He is free to keep it. The law would have to be changed to address requisition. We are so hung up on gun purchases that we ignore the more fundamental fact that gun possession is the problem, whether borrowed, bought, stolen or grandfathered.

* There are cases where the aggressor has been reported to the police by his live-in girlfriend for beatings and threats on her life. A judge has passed a restraining order. Even so, the aggressor is free to buy weapons because he was not actually married to his victim. He was only a live-in boyfriend. The state law forbade only spouses from buying a guy, not live-in boyfriends. This is known as the boy-friend loophole. One may ask: why not change

the law? We've tried but the NRA has fought all such attempts on the ground that confiscating the gun from the abusive boyfriend would deprive him of due process. We need to pass legislation to change this. The question is: do we have the will, the resources and the indignation to confront the NRA and persevere until the law is changed? That remains to be seen.

* In another case the individual manages to get a gun anyway from an unofficial store such as Facebook, or at a gun show, or from a bad-apple store where there are no background checks. We have been at this since President Obama made it one of his crusades.

* In some cases there is a gun relinquishing law, but it is up to a judge to decide whether the accused abuser should relinquish his weapons. Some judges are reluctant to take away the guns on the grounds that domestic abuse does not merit gun confiscation, which is deemed to be Draconian. Apparently, the gun rights of domestic abusers still trump the safety of their threatened significant others. The abuser wins.

* Sometimes it isn't the law that is amiss but its implementation, the will, the perseverance, the commitment, the resources and the dedication to enforce it. Protective restraining orders are token measures, applied weakly and perfunctorily. Some judges do not believe that civil courts should be involved with this issue. According to a newsletter in *The Trace,* the prosecutorial reluctance is biased in favor of the aggressors and against the victims: "In California, a 2005 report prepared for the attorney general found that some judges 'intimidate victims' making it harder for them to obtain protection orders. (See: "Domestic Abusers Frequently Get to Keep their Guns," by Jennifer Mascia, *The Trace*, October 26, 2015).

* Another example of the weak implementation of the law is in the failure to report the facts about the aggressor. Staffers, either through negligence or misguided magnanimity, protect the aggressor by not passing along his information. After the

massacre we learn that the national data bases have no information on the aggressor. Everybody asks after the fact: how was this possible? This was the case with Devin Patrick Kelley, the domestic abuser who killed 26 people during a church service in Sutherland Springs, Tx. The records on him were substantial. Yet he managed to buy four guns in different states over a short period of time.

Domestic violence starts with a live-in partner, but when it explodes into violence it often results in mass shootings. The breadth and scope of the brutality in these cases is of terroristic proportions and typically includes children, relatives and friends of the victim as well. Incidentally, the term "mass shootings" in the title to this chapter is used advisedly. The official definition comes from this source:

> **Everytown** defines a mass shooting as an incident in which four or more people, not including the shooter, are killed with a firearm. The threshold of four fatalities –which is used by the majority of academics and organizations studying mass violence –is derived from a definition of mass murder used in a 2005 FBI report." **HTTPS://EVERYTOWNRESEARCH.ORG/ REPORTS/MASS-SHOOTINGS-ANALYSIS/?NCID=EDLIN KUSHPMG00000313**

Hell hath no fury as that of a disaffected, estranged and rebuffed spousal abuser with a gun. The hatred, the overweening fervor for revenge, the malice is beyond all human bounds. Here are some recent cases.

> July 26, 2014, Saco, ME. Joel Smith kills his wife Heather, their two children and his stepson, before killing himself. The red flags in this case are not from official records, but from the circumstances provided by the father of the killer. Joel was an alcoholic, who was fighting depression; his wife was a drug addict, far gone.

They had been going through dire financial circumstances and he had pointed a gun to his head and threatened to kill himself. The signs that the killings were coming were there. But at least the children could have been saved. **HTTPS://EVERYTOWN-RESEARCH.ORG/REPORTS/MASS-SHOOTINGS-ANALYSIS/?NCID=EDLINKUSHPMG00000313**

December 1, 2014, Morgantown. W.V. Jody Lee Hunt kills four people with a gun he bought from an individual whom he contacted through an ad on Facebook, perfectly legally. He could not have bought a gun through a licensed store because some fifteen years earlier he had been convicted of kidnapping a girlfriend, holding her hostage at gunpoint and had been sentenced to serve ten years. All this background did not help his latest victims. The people he killed were: an ex-girlfriend, her boyfriend, a business rival and his cousin. **HTTPS://EVERYTOWNRESEARCH. ORG/REPORTS/MASS-SHOOTINGS-ANALYSIS/? NCID=EDLINKUSHPMG00000313**

May 29, 2015, Chesterfield County, VA. Stafford Leo Shaw kills his wife Morgan Rogers and their 1-year-old daughter. Then, while evading police he crashes, killing two others before committing suicide. In February he had beat his wife over the head with a gun. She reported him and he was ordered to serve jail time on weekends. She was given a protective order for two years. He could not buy a gun, but Virginia law did not require him to relinquish the gun he already owned and with which he did his killing. **HTTPS://EVERYTOWNRESEARCH.ORG/ REPORTS/MASS-SHOOTINGS-ANALYSIS/?NCID=EDLIN KUSHPMG00000313**

June 29, 2016, Clark County, NV. Jason Dej-Odoum shot and kills his wife Phoukeo at a Walgreens parking lot. Phoukeo had applied for a protective order on June 8, citing threats in the past. The order was denied on the grounds that the threats were not recent. After killing her, Jason went home and killed their three children, ages 9 to15. Then he killed himself. **HTTPS://EVERYTOWNRESEARCH.ORG/REPORTS/ MASS-SHOOTINGS-ANALYSIS/?NCID=EDLINKUSH PMG00000313**

Memorial Day weekend, 2017, Plano, TX. Spencer Hight, estranged husband of 27-year-old Meredith Hight, kills her and seven others as they grilled dinner on the backyard. Spencer was killed by an officer on the scene, which brought the total deaths to nine altogether. https://www.yahoo.com/news/2-deadliest-mass-shootings-common-183556136.html

Rural Mississippi, May 2017. Willie Cory Godbolt, recently estranged husband of Sheena Godbolt, came to the house of Sheena's mother where they were having a cookout and killed Sheena, the mother and other relatives a well as a deputy who responded to the violence. Then he drove to other houses where he killed other members of his wife's family. In all, eight people were killed. He was caught and is awaiting trial. https://www.yahoo.com/news/2-deadliest-mass-shootings-common-183556136.html

On November 5, 2017 Devin Patrick Kelley opened fire on a church service killing 26 persons and injuring 20 others in Sutherland Springs, TX. His domestic-violence conviction had not been entered into the NCIC (National Crime Information Center). His rap sheet should have prevented him from possessing a gun. He had beaten up his ex-wife, had choked her, put a gun on her temple and threatened to kill her. He had beaten up her infant son and broken his skull. He had spent time in a mental institution in New Mexico where he had hoarded guns and threatened his military superiors. He had been convicted of cruelty to animals. All this and more was a matter of record. How could we have failed so miserably in acting upon data that could have prevented him from killing people? The answer reveals our worst nightmares. The following account, quoted from TIME magazine, presents the dismal details.

This was hardly an isolated error. According to a Florida International University report obtained by TIME, the military mishandled roughly 1,300 domestic violence cases between 2004 and 2012, including misclassification that allowed abusers to go unreported in the NCIC.

'There are thousands of cases that have been misclassified," says Eric Carpenter, an associate professor at FIU and a former Army lawyer who spent years sifting through military court-martial data.'

The problem runs deeper than poor record keeping. Federal law prohibits anyone convicted of domestic violence or subject to a domestic-violence restraining order from owning a gun. But spotty enforcement can allow abusers to fall through the cracks. While 28 states and Washington, D.C., have laws prohibiting domestic batterers from buying or possessing firearms, only 14 require them to give up the guns they already own.

TIME, November 20, 2017. **Time, November 20, 2017**.

These are not isolated cases. A broader perspective of this phenomenon is provided by this summary of mass shootings in the United States by *Everytown*.

- From 2009-2016 in the U.S., there have been 156 mass shootings— incidents in which four or more people were shot and killed, not including the shooter. These incidents resulted in 1,187 victims shot: 848 people were shot and killed, and 339 people were shot and injured. In addition, 66 perpetrators killed themselves after a mass shooting, and another 17 perpetrators were shot and killed by responding law enforcement.
- The majority of mass shootings—54 percent of cases—were related to domestic or family violence.
- Mass shootings significantly impacted children: 25 percent of mass shooting fatalities (211) were children. This is primarily

driven by mass shootings related to domestic or family violence, in which over 40 percent of fatalities were children.

- In nearly half of the shootings—42 percent of cases—the shooter exhibited warning signs before the shooting indicating that he posed a danger to himself or others. These red flags included acts, attempted acts, or threats of violence towards oneself or others; violations of protective orders; or evidence of ongoing substance abuse.

- More than one-third of the shootings—34 percent—involved a shooter who was prohibited from possessing firearms.

- Only ten percent of incidents took place in "gun-free zones", or areas where civilians are prohibited from carrying firearms and there is not a regular armed law enforcement presence (armed security guards, for example). The vast majority of incidents—63 percent—took place entirely in private homes. **HTTPS://EVERYTOWNRESEARCH.ORG/REPORTS/ MASS-SHOOTINGS-ANALYSIS/?NCID=EDLINKUSH PMG00000313**

CHAPTER 9

Gun Decisions

● ● ●

IF YOU ARE A CRIMINAL, a thief, burglar, drug dealer, or killer for hire, then a gun is indispensable for you and this chapter does not apply to you – you probably have an arsenal already anyway. But also, if you are not a criminal, and your job and your travels take you through dangerous environments and circumstances, you too may need a gun.

But if you are an ordinary American not involved in illegal dangerous activities and have no compelling need for a gun, and you are contemplating having one just to have one, then you should read and weigh the potential risks of having a gun. A gun could save your life, but it could also give you much grief. It behooves you to know the pros and cons. Statistics show that gun buyers are moved by visceral reactions and go half-cocked to the gun stores after a massacre. They claim they are buying for self-defense, but many of them don't bother to take lessons to learn to handle the guns and they are not respectful of the dangers of having a gun in the home. They keep the gun in an unsafe place fully loaded with the lock mechanism off where children can get hold of them. They think nothing can happen to them. They don't do their homework; they make little effort to stay informed and learn what is happening to others. They don't read, don't even watch the TV news and are likely to become part of the tragic gun statistics documented at the end of the chapter. Here is a simple framework to help you think about your decisions. To keep it simple, I shall consider only two environments, S and U for safe and unsafe. You have two options: G, get a gun; or X, don't. The four possible contingencies that apply are: SG, SX, UG and UX.

SG: The environment is safe and crime free, and yet the individual gets a gun. Why? Perhaps he grew up around guns. Perhaps he is a gun lover and is predisposed to have a gun –for psychological comfort, adornment or amulet.

Or, perhaps he is not a gun lover, but has been persuaded that it is a good idea to have a gun for self-defense, just in case the need should ever arise. Self-defense, after all, involves no belligerence, no ill will to others and is extolled as an honorable right, as an eminently justifiable protection, a noble call to arms. It is so morally defensible that society virtually puts a halo over the gun, giving it its blessings. What's there not to like?

Think again. The gun introduces risks into the environment which may not be worthwhile. If the environment is safe, as assumed, why endanger it? If there are children in his household, the risk for tragedies is multiplied several times over. See Chapter 12 for a section covering guns and children. These accidents are not uncommon and are among the most bizarre tragedies in the human condition. Some defy the laws of probability. Of course, the decision maker himself could be at risk of untoward outcomes simply because guns can be very tricky and deadly. They are merciless with human error and negligence.

SX: this is the safe situation, but without a gun. A gun averter would definitely choose this option. For him, introducing a gun into this safe situation is counterproductive; it spoils the harmless environment with its threat of accidents. He would heed the warnings that the gun lover ignored and remain gun free.

But what does the gun averter have to say about the self-defense argument? He doesn't buy it. For him, self-defense is not what it is hyped up to be. He sees self-defense as a glorified lie, as an excuse to have a gun, as a pretext the NRA uses to sell more guns. If self-defense were real, if it paid off, if it had a fraction of the virtues that are ascribed to it, we would see proof of it in foiled attacks, in thousands of defeats for the criminals and victories for the defenders. But the numbers that the authorities provide, such as the Violence Policy Center, do not show self-defense to be significant. The data do not support self-defense. Statistically, self-defense is a myth. For example, according to an article by Michael McLaughlin in the *Huffington Post*, "Using Guns in Self-Defense is Rare, Study Finds" (June 17, 2015), there were 258 justifiable homicides in 2012, compared to 8,342 murders by guns.

Also, gun averters are not lured by heroic fantasies. They are deaf to the call to arms. They see gun lovers arming themselves to the gills to fight the windmills of their dreams. Gun averters prefer to stay back in the dull unglamorous world of the unarmed and opt for life without guns.

UG: this is the war zone. Here we have a dangerous environment and the gun is justified. The individual should prepare to become a warrior. He may need to shoot his way out of trouble. He should train himself well and be careful. Good luck.

No doubt, a gun lover would adjust better to this contingency than a gun averter. The gun averter would be a miserable fish out of water. Many men in law enforcement make a living in this world and for that they deserve our gratitude. Most of them are cut out for that life and find compensation and gratification in it. Some men are inspired and roused by the clarion call to action and adventure. Daydreams of chivalry are evoked, imbuing gun lovers with a surge of interventionism as they rush as warriors and defenders to save the world. From this contingency the dawn of gun adventures rises.

UX This unsafe environment without guns has its own peculiar dangers. You could be invaded at home or accosted by a burglar on the street. You could witness someone being brutalized, but you can do nothing because you have no gun. How do the gun averters deal with the threat of these possibilities? They deal with them rationally, probabilistically and philosophically. They will take all necessary precautions to not tempt danger, avoiding certain hours, certain places and avoiding traveling alone. They will call 911. They are prepared to run and hide; they will avoid heroics. They will give up their valuables; they will plead; and they will just hope for the best. But they will not get a gun. It is a risk they are willing to take. They would prefer, of course, that we change the environment and reduce the threat by taking the gun out of the picture as so many civilized countries around the world have already done. They would prefer to reach a compromise with the gun lovers: keep your guns, but give up some of your gun rights so the rest of us can enjoy a safer life.

Gun lovers, on the other hand, probably detest UX more than any other contingency. The mere thought of being caught in a dangerous situation without their gun is a nightmare of unbearable torment. Think of it, what could be worse to a gun lover than to have his gun nearby in sight, but out of reach, while being threatened by a bad guy with a gun?

A Decision-Making Game. The behavior of gun averters and gun lovers can be explored by making up games that would show the way they would place their bets if they were maximizing their utility in uncertain situations. But these are just intellectual fantasies. I have played around with these tables, changing the probabilities and changing the investments, engaging in speculative scenarios, which I will spare the reader. The games have been useful and have helped me realize something important. I believe that people tend to adhere tenaciously to their biases and to their inherent nature. A gun lover will tend to remain a gun lover and a gun averter will tend to remain gun averse. Necessity may force me to arm myself temporarily; if, for example, there was a sudden spate of home invasions in my area. But it would not make me a gun lover.

What would it take to make me change? In my musings through the game I would change the probability of the scenarios, but every time I was able to change my investments to countervail the probability and I would remain gun averse. The same, I believe, would be true for a gun lover. It is not easy to change habits and addictions.

This is discouraging for someone who wants to change our taste for guns, but not fatally so. I believe that personal cataclysms can change us. Losing a child because of your gun negligence must be a wrenching experience of unrelenting recrimination and grief. Such an excruciating experience could be compelling and change your habits more effectively than speculative game scenarios. The question is: why should we wait to experience such a calamity before changing? Is there another way?

Humans are who they are because of their trajectories through life. The experiences they live in their own flesh and blood are their school. They learn that fire is hot by getting burned. But some of us learn the bitter lessons of life vicariously, by witnessing the experiences of others. We shouldn't have to get burned ourselves to learn. Information is a critical factor for living safely and wisely. That is why it is appalling that we don't seem to learn from the gun tragedies that beset us in America day after day. We destine ourselves to experience them. Here, then, are some parting observations about probabilities and about information on the subject of guns. The vagaries of fate are indeed inscrutable.

On Probabilities. Probabilities are like the winds of fate that blow us hither and yon. We try to sail them. Sometimes we even succeed at it. We use them to advantage and we think we are in control. But sometimes probabilities can ridicule our mathematics and our expected values with flukes and outliers.

Here is an example. Suppose we flipped a coin six times in a row. You would anticipate that the results would be varied, if not 3H and 3T, maybe 4H and 2T, but certainly not all Hs. If you did get 6 Hs, you would be understandably flummoxed and biased towards heads. You would ask yourself: what happened? Does this result prove the coin is not fair? Not necessarily. Statisticians would tell you that six flips are insufficient to make a decision. The laws of probability do not preclude that from happening. It is possible that, while the coin is fair, you could still get such a fluke, even though its probability is very, very low. But so long as the probability is not zero, it does not preclude flukes. It is these flukes that we have to worry about, especially when it comes to guns.

Here is one example of a horrible fluke that occurred on January1, 2015.

Veronica J. Rutledge, 29, was shopping at Walmart with her 2-year old son and three nieces in Hayden, Idaho. Her young son managed to unzip the special gun compartment in the woman's purse where the weapon was kept while she was looking at clothing. He fired the gun and shot his mother in the head, killing her instantly. https://www.washingtonpost.com/news/morning-mix/wp/2014/12/31/the-inside-story-of-how-an-idaho-toddler-shot-his-mom-at-wal-mart/

According to the father-in-law the mother was not careless. She handled guns responsibly and took every precaution. The gun was within two zippered compartments. This is one of those unfortunate flukes that should be widely disseminated and borne in mind when considering owning a gun.

But there is more. Accidents abound around guns. There are so many gun accidents that we could fit them into a wide range of categories. Some are ludicrous and occur because of recklessness or stupidity. Fate had little to do with them. There are cases, believe it or not, where dogs shot the guns, as in the following account by Louis Klarevas http://www.huffingtonpost.com/louis-klarevas/dog-shooting-accidents_b_4110822.html

A quick internet search uncovered at least 17 shootings by man's supposed best friend since 1980. (Not to be left out, a cat was responsible for knocking over a loaded handgun, causing it to fire a 9 mm cartridge into a Michigan man's torso.)

The vast majority of these shootings (15 out of 17) occurred in Southern and Midwestern states -- jurisdictions with traditionally lax gun laws. Three canine cappings occurred in Florida alone, including one earlier this year in Sebring. In that "accident," an investigating police officer reported that Gregory Dale Lanier's dog "kicked his unloaded .380 pistol causing it to fire and the bullet to strike his leg." To Lanier's surprise, the gun turned out to be loaded after all. (And it came as an additional surprise to Lanier that his firearm was a 9mm handgun, not a .380.)

Not funny, and sadly tragic, are the staggering number of accidents involving children. Normally, we learn from our mistakes and the mistakes of others. But this assumes that we are perceptive and care to know what's going on in the world. This assumes that we have curiosity, that we get our information from reliable sources, that we read newspapers and magazines and that we watch the evening news. This is how we learn about the danger to avoid and this is how we wise up. But some people are clueless about the world around them and make no effort to be informed. Young people, in particular, seem to be tuned in only to what interests them: to rock, sports, and violent movies. They don't read newspapers and they don't even watch the TV news. Change can only take place if people are touched and influenced by information. But if they close their windows, or shut their eyes and ears, or withdraw into their shells, they are impervious to influences. It is difficult to inspire change in this people. They are unreachable. Probabilities for them are imponderable.

Others are informed, but they do not process information intelligently, or they just don't care. They dismiss as irrelevant whatever happens to others. It is as if they said: that's them, not me. All the warnings about the harm of such things as drugs, smoking, texting while driving and guns simply bounce off because these people are convinced that they can beat the probabilities.

We cannot give up on them. We have to continue to reach them and continue to pass the word for safety and common sense. For these reasons information and education about guns has to be an ongoing campaign. It is in good measure the reason that compels me to write this book. We need to stay on focus and keep tabs on the gun killings and perform post mortems, going over all the details. Why did they happen? Where did we fail? How could they have been prevented? How did the guns fit into the tragedies? This goes not only for the gun accidents, but for the wanton killings as well.

Aside from our individual decisions as to whether to own a gun or not, we should also look beyond ourselves and look at the broader picture and contemplate the nature of the country we live in. What is our conclusion about guns in America? After processing so many murders, so many massacres, so many accidents, how do we feel about the accessibility of guns? How do we feel about safety in our country? Should we go on like this?

I suspect that the majority of Americans are not content with things as they are. We suffer from gun pollution. But they don't know what to do. They don't see how it is possible to change our laws and our way of life. If this is indeed the case, then there is hope for us. Just keep the discontent alive and turn it into action when the time comes.

CHAPTER 10

International Comparisons

● ● ●

WE ALL DIE; THAT'S NOTHING new. But how and why we die is of concern. When deaths by guns are as high as they are in the U.S. it behooves us to ask: Are we alone in this? How do we compare with similar countries? And how can we carry out a meaningful comparison? In this chapter I will provide my own adjustment for population differences and differences due to gun culture. The usual method is by reporting the number of gun deaths per 100,000, but this is not very revealing. I will present a method that decomposes the effects of population and gun culture. Here are the variables of interest:

Definitions	US figures for year 2010
G, the number of annual deaths by guns	G = 32,163
P, the total population	P = 309,326,295
g = G/P, the rate of gun deaths	g = 0.000104

Notice that G, the number of gun deaths, can be represented as the area of a rectangle with length P and height g, for a total area of G = gP as in Fig 10.1.

Notice also that Figure 10.1 shows the number of deaths of a smaller country with a lower rate of gun deaths. This is indicated by the smaller shaded rectangle. The question is how do we compare the two countries with respect to gun deaths? The obvious thing to do is to subtract the two areas, but this does not break down the reasons for the differences.

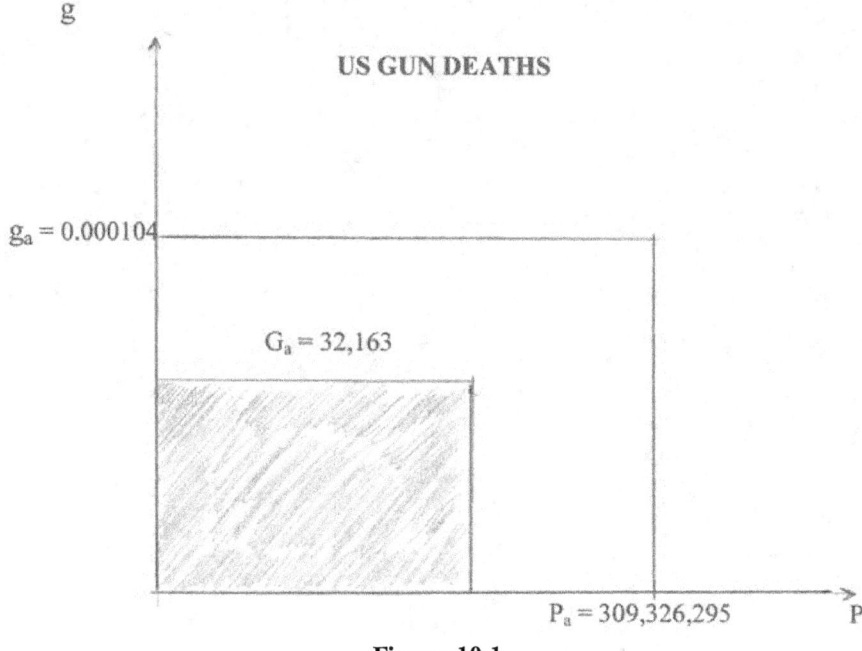

g

US GUN DEATHS

$g_a = 0.000104$

$G_a = 32,163$

$P_a = 309,326,295$ P

Figure 10.1

Specifically, the number of gun deaths in France for year 2010 was 1,736 while in the US we had 32,163. So, the difference in gun deaths is: 32,163 – 1,736 = 30,427. But what do we make of this huge difference? The countries have substantially different populations; the US has 309 million, while France has 65 million. It is also true that we have a lot more guns throughout the population and different attitudes about guns. Is it possible to correct for the difference in population and gun culture? To this we now turn.

Instead of dealing with two specific countries, US and France, I shall now generalize to two unspecified countries A and B. Figure 10.2 shows the gun deaths for countries A and B. The gun deaths for country A is the big rectangle with area: $g_a P_a$. Country B's area is the small shaded rectangle with area $G_B = g_b P_b$. Interestingly, we see that if we subtract

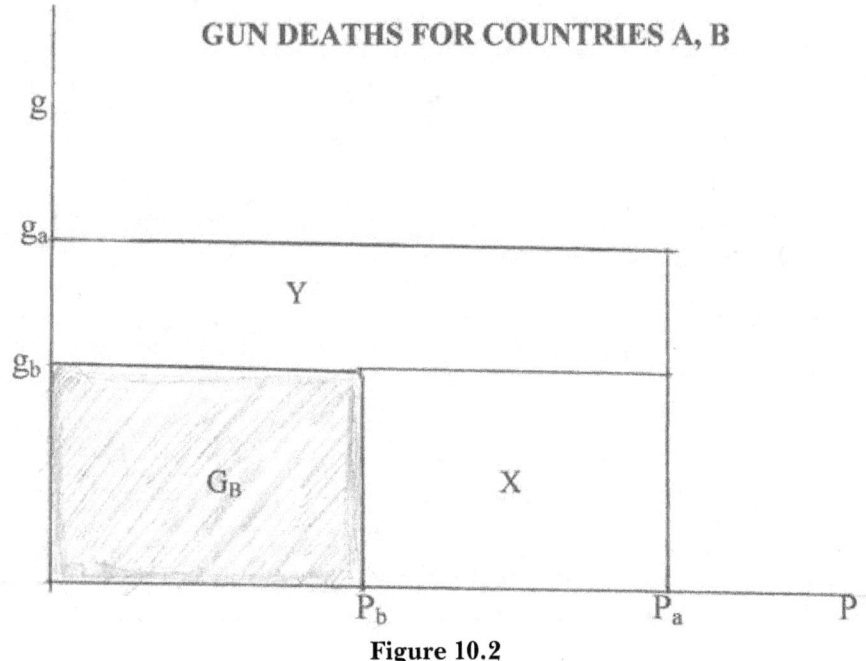

Figure 10.2

the small rectangle G_B from the big one, G_A, we are left with two areas X and Y, thus:

(10.1) $G_A - G_B = X + Y$

The X rectangle represents the adjustment due to population and the Y rectangle is the adjustment due to differences in gun culture. Let me show why this is so.

Let's ask: what would have been the number of deaths in country B if it had retained its gun death rate g_b, but had the same population as A? I designate this number of deaths with an asterisk to show it is a potential number. Its calculation is given by the rectangle:

(10.2) $G^*(B/P_a) = g_b P_a$

By looking at Figure 10.2 we can see that this is also equal to:

$$(10.3) \quad G^*(B/P_a) = G_B + X$$

Clearly, the difference between the (potential B) and the (actual B) is X:

$$(10.4) \quad G^*(B/P_a) - G_B = X$$

X is, therefore, the population adjustment component we have been seeking. It is what we need to add to country B in order to determine how many more gun deaths it would have had if its population had been equal to that of country A. We can also visualize it as: $X = g_b(P_a - P_b)$.

Having adjusted B for the population difference with A, there still remains the gun factor to consider. This is the remaining residual which we can derive by subtracting $G^*(B/P_a)$ from the actual gun deaths of country A to get:

$$(10.5) \quad G_A - G^*_{B/Pa} = g_a P_A - g_b P_A$$

Again, by referring to Figure 10.2 we see that this difference is also equal to

$$(10.6) \quad G_A - G^*_{B/Pa} = Y$$

In other words, Y is what still remains after subtracting the potential, population-adjusted deaths of country B. We can also visualize it as: $Y = (g_a - g_b)P_a$.

By substituting (9.3) into (9.6) and rearranging terms we get (10.1) again,

$$(10.1) \quad G_a - G_b = X + Y$$

as was to be shown. In sum, the difference in gun deaths between countries A and B is, indeed, the sum of two components X and Y which account for both population differences and gun related differences.

I shall now proceed to identify specific countries and use real data to measure the concepts just explained. Table 10.1 below introduces the population and the gun deaths for selected European countries. All the variables of the model are now given flesh and blood. As expected, the table confirms that the US leads on the number of gun deaths by staggering amounts. While it is true that we are the largest country, it is also true that population alone does not account for the differences in gun deaths.

Table 10.1. for year 2010

COUNTRY	POPULATION, P	GUN DEATHS, G	GUN RATE, g = G/P per 1000
U.S.	309,326,295	32,163	0.1040
France	65,027,142	1,736	0.0267
Germany	81,776,930	819	0.0100
Canada	34,005,274	781	0.0229
U.K.	62,766,365	145	0.0023
Australia	22,030,000	232	0.00001

Population Source: http://datatopics.worldbank.org/hnp/popestimates#
Gun Source: gunpolicy.org/firearms/compare/194/total number of gun deaths/
31.66.69.12

In Table 10.2 below I present the computed values for X and Y and the values for gun deaths for each of the countries.

INTERPRETATION. Here is how to read the numbers in Table 10.2. Consider France in the first row. The US had 30,427 more gun deaths than France. But if France had had the same population as the US and its own rate of gun deaths, there would have been 6,522 more gun deaths in France. Hence, the population adjustment raises the gun deaths for France from 1,736 to 6,522. This adjustment accounts for only 21% of the total difference between the two countries. The remainder is

Table 10.2 GUN DEATH COMPARISONS

Countries	ACTUAL	DEATHS		ADJUSTMENTS	
	US	2nd Country	Difference	$X_{population}$	Y_{guns}
US-France	32,163	1,736	30,427	6,522 21%	23,905 79%
US-German	32,163	819	31,344	2,279 7%	29,065 93%
US-Canada	32,163	781	31,382	6,323 20%	25,059 80%
US-UK	32,163	145	32,018	570 2%	31,448 98%
US-Austral	32,163	232	31,931	3,025 9%	28,906 91%

the gun component Y, which is 23,905 gun deaths and is the major factor for the difference between the two countries; it explains 79% of the difference between the US and France. A similar interpretation holds for the other countries. Consistently, the gun culture is the greatest factor in gun deaths between the US and comparable countries.

A Final Note. We can gather the data and go to the trouble of presenting it and making comparisons to show that the US is out of line with its gun violence. Guns are a disaster of our own making. Most people would be alarmed and embarrassed by these shameful statistics and would want to do something about them. But, remarkably, many Americans don't care and simply ask: so what? They don't like being compared to other countries. They want to keep America as it is, guns and all, warts and all. If we don't like it, we are invited to move to the countries with the fewer guns. That's their solution to the problem: slay the messenger, banish the critics.

These butt-headed Americans act as if they are proud to be wrong. The stigma of being the most violent nation among civilized western countries gives them no shame. For them the guns are worth it.

Well, who cares what they think? The rest of us are going to have to save the country without them. The situation reminds me of those cases when a gravely ill child falls through the legal cracks. He needs a transfusion, a bone marrow transplant and chemo-therapy. Unfortunately, the child is under the guardianship of narrow minded people who oppose these treatments on religious grounds or stupidity. Unfortunately, they have the power and the authority to prevent the treatment. Their warped sense of values endangers the wellbeing of the child. They are proud of their beliefs. The death of the child is a small price for upholding what they believe to be right. If it comes to their beliefs or the child's life, the child loses.

If the situation only involved the parents' own body, one would be tempted to just leave them to their faith and their own fate. Keep your beliefs and die. But when their belief involves the rights of others, it is a different matter. They should not be allowed to kill by their stupidity. Sadly, in this case the child is the US itself, which suffers from an addiction to guns. Its wellbeing should not be left to the authority of the gun lovers any more than that poor child should be left to the ignorance and intransigence of his parents. Gun lovers should not have the right to intrude on caring for a sick America. For most Americans the country comes first. They don't love guns that blindly. Gun rights at the expense of so much violence are simply not worth it.

Finally, another very useful purpose for the international comparison is to show that it is possible to live with fewer guns. Look at France! Look at England! How do they do it? How can they manage to live with so little gun violence, with less mayhem and fewer shootings? These countries show palpably that gun reduction and stricter controls are not quixotic quests or dreams of the impossible. They are attainable realities. If others can do it, why can't we?

CHAPTER 11

Why Guns are Cheap

● ● ●

WE ARE IN A GUN glut due to cheap guns. Their prices do not reflect the true costs of the damages they cause society. The gun manufacturers and gun dealers ignore the *negative externalities of guns* (explained below) and do not help defray the collateral incidental damage that guns cause. In this chapter I will show the free rides that guns get.

Let's begin with an individual gun owner. He derives "utility" from the possession and use of his gun; or, as laymen would put it, he gets pleasure and satisfaction from his gun. However, because the gun and the ammo are not free, the individual's utility is constrained by costs. His consumption is tempered by what he can afford. In order to see how the two things, utility and cost, interface, I will start by considering a situation of free ammunition. Then I will add the costs one by one and note their effect. The obvious costs will come first, then the more complicated ones of unintended consequences.

Free Ammo. If bullets were free we would have only two things to consider: the utility and the cost of the guns. These are shown in Fig. 11.1. The utility is shown by the curve U while the cost of the gun itself is designated by the flat line K. This is flat because it is a fixed cost, a one-time thing; it does not vary with use. Whether you fire it every day or you store it and never use it, it does not change what you paid for it. Also, the utility for the gun itself has already been accounted for and is designated by U_o in the graph. If the gun owner merely held the gun and never fired it, he would be at the point over the origin, $X = 0$; his cost would be K, what he paid for it; and his utility would be U_o.

But, of course, if he did fire the gun, then he would derive extra utility above and beyond mere ownership. His utility would then vary according to how much shooting he did. A good measure of this usage is the rounds of ammo he would use, X. As he used more ammo, his utility would rise from point U_o. The shape of the utility curve shown here is traditional for economic analysis.

Because we are assuming for now that the bullets are free, the gun owner is unrestricted and the question arises: how much ammo would he use at a zero price? We assume that he would want to maximize his Net Utility, N, which in this case would be:

(11.1) $N = U - K$

Graphically, N is the gap between the curve U and the line K. To maximize N is to find its widest point. That point occurs in Fig. 10.1 at X_{max}. He would fire away until he got sick of firing, until extra shooting would add no more pleasure, until subsequent firing diminished his utility. In brief, he would fire away until he reached the point X_{max}.

When Ammo Is Not Free. But if the bullets were not free, his firing would be constrained. So, let us introduce a non-zero price **p** for the ammo. In this case, the cost function is no longer a flat line but an upsloping one. Its equation is:

(11.2) $C_1 = K + pX$ where p is the price per round of ammo

The cost line now rises from K, from the value of the gun, and it rises depending on how much ammo is used. Also, whether the line rises steeply or gradually depends entirely on the price p. If p were $20 per bullet the cost line would be steep. In any case, whether p is low or high, we should note that when p is non-zero, p impacts the maximization process. The gun owner's Net Utility is now altered to:

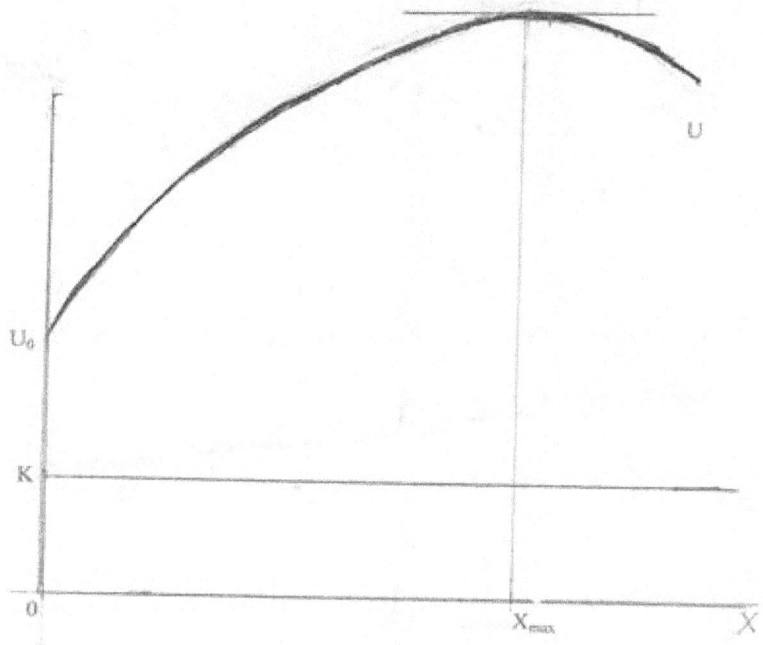

Fig. 11.1

(11.3) $N = U - C_1 = U - (K + pX)$

Net Utility is no longer the gap between U and K, but between U and the cost line C_1. From Fig.11.2 below we see that Net Utility is a maximum at a lower value than before. The new maximum now occurs at X_1.

The introduction of cost, even when this is low, reduces gun usage. If the ammo were more expensive, this would increase the slope of the cost line and this, in turn, would push the point X_1 further back, making the gap between X_1 and X_{max} greater. The lesson here is that cost always changes behavior. If something is free, it does not restrain use; it does not force us to economize. But if it is not free, we retrench consumption.

Spillovers and Externalities. Thus far we have considered the simplest costs, the cost of the gun itself and the ammo, the sort of obvious

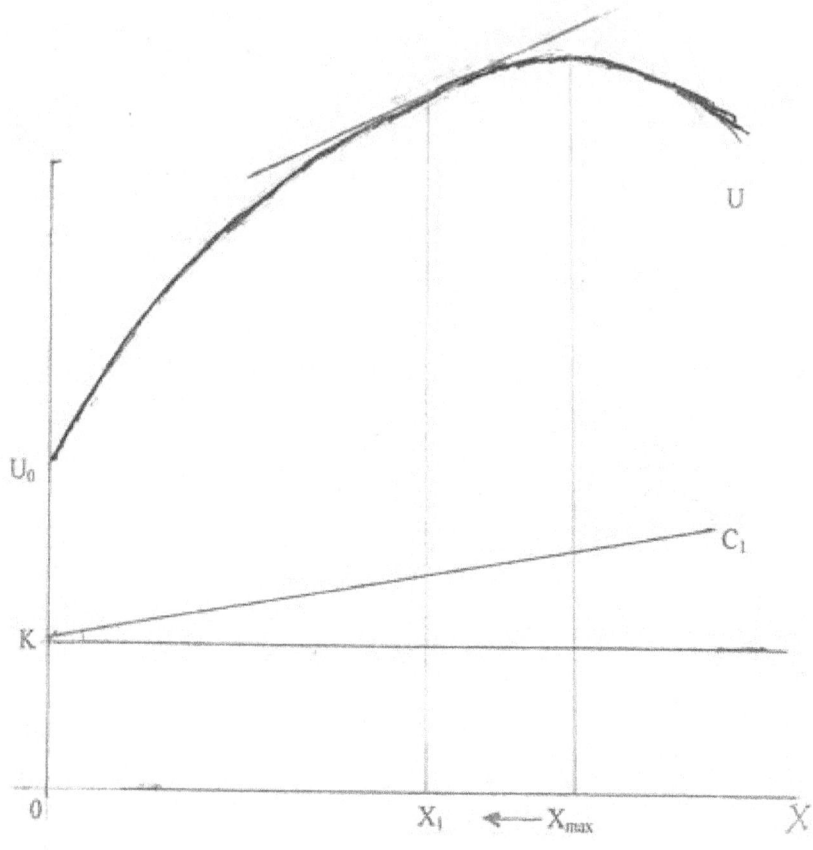

Fig. 11.2

costs that leave a paper trail that can be backed up with data, with receipts and invoices. But there are other more insidious costs that are difficult to quantify because they include imponderables with no paper trail, such as the damage done to third parties. These are called **spill-over costs** and **negative externalities** in Economics.

Externalities are not always bad. There are positive and beneficial externalities. To clarify the concept, suppose your home backed up to an old tenement with rundown property full of squatters. Suppose a developer buys that property and razes the old buildings and turns the land into a golf course. Now your house backs up to an attractive peaceful landscape. That is a positive externality to you. It cost you nothing. You were a third party who benefited from the transaction of two other parties and they cannot charge you for the benefit that spilled over to you.

On the other hand, a negative externality will harm you. The best example of a negative externality is pollution, pollution to the environment, or of the air, or of our waterways. If you lived downwind from a plant that spewed out ash and smoke, you would suffer from a negative externality.

In the case of negative externalities, there is redress through a number of mechanisms for the afflicted third party. In some instances it is possible for the parties involved to negotiate compensation between themselves, without involving the government. More often, the government has to intervene and pass laws to protect the afflicted third party, which is often none other than society at large, its lungs, its land, its flora, its fauna, its air, its rivers, etc. What is certain is that were it not for government control, the polluting firms would continue polluting and pay nothing for the damages they cause. The firms would have no incentive to develop cleaner or safer manufacturing methods.

In some instances you can sue for damages, but whether you get anything after long and expensive litigation is uncertain. Negative externalities take us out of the realm of Economics into a fluid, wild legal world which is still unchartered, especially so in the case of guns. We have not gotten even to first base in resolving the externalities of the gun market. Government is involved, but only in a very superficial way; the laws are porous and without teeth. Moreover, by now the gun market has been politicized. The gun industry operates in an environment protected by powerful political forces. The gun lobby uses the Second Amendment to sabotage change and to hold onto things as they are.

But what if the guns and the bullets were not so cheap? What if they were hard to buy? What if a single bullet cost $72? And what if the cheapest and simplest gun cost over $1,000? What if the license to carry a gun was fifty times what it is now? What if we required liability insurance for guns? What if the penalty for possessing a gun without insurance or without a license was $3,000? What if the gun manufacturers and the gun dealers could be sued and made liable for the damages that they contributed to, as the cigarette manufacturers were? What if we taxed heavily the ammo per round? What if the protection that schools and colleges have to incur in detection devices and greater security could be passed to the gun dealers? What if the Surgeon General of the United States declared guns harmful to the general health of the country?

All these questions hint at ways to internalize the social costs. If they were ever internalized, the prices for the guns and for the ammo would reflect the true cost to society and would be much higher. The cost curve in Fig. 11.2 would shift and rise with a vengeance. It would probably be a mean cubic of varying slopes with pronounced inflection points that would mark its soaring segments. At present the cost curves for guns are unburdened and exempt from their externalities and reality. It is as if nobody was being killed through all the firings, as if the guns and the bullets that kill people had absolutely nothing to do with their deaths. There is no accountability for the harm that guns cause.

All of the above cost transferences are unthinkable today. Nothing can be done at the moment because the NRA, fearing such measures, has beaten us to the punch politically. They have advertised and they have run PR campaigns to rally people around their flag. This has raised their costs and eaten into their profits a little. But it has been offset by the increased membership of the NRA. They have raised more contributions and have been able to lobby more politicians. They are fighting for the mind and soul of Americans and, all in all, they have grown and have become stronger. State legislatures across the country are passing gun laws that extend the places where guns can be taken, that extend the way guns are carried –concealed in some states, open carry in others. Cities are mandating its citizens to have a gun at home.

The passivity of gun critics is part of the NRA's strength. This will have to change. Those of us who decry the dominion of the gun must rise to condemn it, must argue against it and rally more and more people against the gun. When we become a powerful political bloc, we will elect the right people and bring about change in our political structure. That is what it will take to make those cost curves rise and shift and bring America to a sane civilized point of equilibrium with guns.

Unfortunately, I don't believe we are ready. Americans still need to be better informed, better educated and more introspective on the issue of guns. They need to think, to examine situations critically and debunk the fallacies and myths that the NRA puts out. The gun people may have the guns, the money, and the political clout. They certainly have the dead bodies, but they don't have the logic.

CHAPTER 12

Gun Irresponsibility

● ● ●

GUNS ARE DANGEROUS. THE THREAT of death that emits out of the dark tunnel of a gun barrel sends me a scary morbid wave that is slightly nauseating. I've kept them away from me for my entire life of 80 years. But others think nothing of it. Guns don't scare them. The death associated with them is a distant abstraction that happens to others, whether it'd be murder, suicide or accident. It is not their concern. People gainsay the danger of guns and look the other way like the piano player at a brothel who blots out of his mind what is going on upstairs.

I understand that the manufacturers and retailers need to be impervious to my qualms or they could not be in the gun business. They probably tell themselves that they are serving a noble purpose by supplying a needed item which is perfectly legal. The end users, the gun buyers, surely have their own rationalizations that shield them from the fear that deadly things impart. And so, with the dangers of the gun dismissed, the gun owners proceed with their deadly gun in hand comfortably, confidently and inured to its dangers. They become irresponsible. Their irresponsibility ranges all the way from carelessness and absentmindedness, to recklessness and ultimately to criminality.

Carelessness is the most benign level of irresponsibility. No premeditation, no malice is involved. Nevertheless, its damage is very real and substantial. It causes many unnecessary deaths, often of innocent people, including children. The unsafe handling of guns is the most common example. This includes leaving them loaded around the house with easy access to children. To show how pervasive this is, I expand on this in the section below entitled "Of Guns and Children."

Recklessness is more serious. Here there may not be any malice or premeditation but there is culpability and there are penalties for it under the law. One instance of this is horsing around and threatening others by gesturing with guns; aiming it at someone without shooting; or shooting it randomly in the air without aiming it at anyone. Other instances are more subtle; they entail no gestures or threats but they are reckless nevertheless because they exhibit no prudence, no common sense. The case that comes to mind here is the mother of Adam Lanza, the teenager who went on a killing rampage at the Sandy Hook Elementary School in Connecticut, on December 14, 2012. She should have known better than to have an arsenal of deadly weapons and to train her unstable son in the use of them. She paid dearly for her misjudgment as she was the first person he killed before he went out on his rampage. All of which brings to mind the brutally honest lesson of a Spanish proverb that says: *Grow horns; they'll poke your eyes out someday.*

Criminality is the gravest level of irresponsibility. This involves violating written statues, such as carrying a gun without a permit, possession of a gun if you are a felon, giving or lending a gun to a minor, selling a gun without following the legal procedures required. The so-called "straw sales" is a prime example of this and is dealt with at greater length in another section to this chapter.

OF GUNS AND CHILDREN.

Accidents involving children are so bizarre that they seem like bad fiction. They are tragic and emotionally wrenching, but their cause is always the adult who owns the gun. How can we rationalize being victims of a tot who got hold of a gun, who did not know what a gun was, or what it was used for? And yet, he pulled the trigger and his sibling or his mother died. The killer is an angel, not a villain. It shouldn't have happened. Nobody willed it. Yet it happened. Sometimes the killing takes place in a home which is an altar of peace where everyone is church-going and God-loving, where murder and killings are unimaginable. But a child gets hold of a gun, the gun just goes poof and a life ends on the spot and kills, fulfilling the gun's prophecy. These deaths should be hyped and rubbed in until they are etched into the soul of all gun owners until more of them take heed. To bring the point home I shall cite some recent cases from: http://kidshootings.blogspot.com/

SATURDAY, JUNE 7, 2014

3 year old Missouri girl killed in accidental shooting. A coroner has ruled the shooting death of a 3-year-old Joplin girl was an accident. Her 6-year-old brother was in the room with her but the authorities cannot say who shot the girl. It appears that she did not shoot herself.

Every gun in the hands of a child must first pass through the hands of an adult.

Posted by Kid Shootings HYPERLINK "http://www.blogger.com/profile/10362802485218403408" at 5:28 PM

FRIDAY, MAY 30, 2014

6 year old Florida boy shoots grandfather with assault rifle

A 6 year old Florida boy got his hands on an AK-47 assault type rifle that was left on a table and accidentally shot and killed his grandfather with the gun.

Posted by Kid Shootings HYPERLINK "http://www.blogger.com/profile/10362802485218403408" at 5:00 AM

MONDAY, MAY 19, 2014

5 year old son of North Carolina law enforcement officer injures himself with father's gun

A 5-year-old son of a deputy in North Carolina is recovering after he shot himself with his father's service weapon over the weekend.

Posted by Kid Shootings HYPERLINK "http://www.blogger.com/profile/10362802485218403408" at 10:37 AM

SUNDAY, MAY 18, 2014

4 year old Indiana boy shot with gun found at home

In yet another "accidental" shooting by a toddler. A 4-year-old boy was fatally shot while holding his parents' gun at his home in Merrillville, Indiana, police said.

Posted by Kid Shootings HYPERLINK "http://www.blogger.com/profile/10362802485218403408" at 9:09 AM

TUESDAY, MAY 13, 2014

16 year old Oregon boy shot to death while sitting in car

Officials said the 16-year-old, Lazaro Lizandro Fuentes Burgos, was shot while he sat in a 1994 Nissan Sentra. Neighbors heard shots around 1:40 a.m., but police weren't notified of the shooting for about an hour. Burgos lived in Southeast Portland's Lents neighborhood and has no known gang ties or drug ties.

Posted by Kid Shootings HYPERLINK "http://www.blogger.com/profile/10362802485218403408" at 5:39 PM

11 year old Oklahoma boy shoots grandmother

An 11-year-old has been arrested in a shooting at a south Tulsa apartment complex near 79th Street and South Sheridan Avenue. Police say a 50-year-old woman was shot in the back of the head around 4 p.m. Monday at Ridgemont Apartments.

Posted by Kid Shootings HYPERLINK "http://www.blogger.com/profile/10362802485218403408" at 5:37 PM

9 year old New Jersey girl shot outside of grandparents' home

A nine-year-old girl is hospitalized after she was shot three times in Trenton on Monday afternoon.

It happened around 3 p.m. on the 200 block of Bellevue Avenue.

Struck by gunfire playing on the sidewalk outside her grandparents' Trenton home, a nine-year-old girl was hit three times by a spray of bullets police believe were intended for someone else.

Posted by Kid Shootings HYPERLINK "http://www.blogger.com/profile/10362802485218403408" at 5:34 PM

As children get older they become less and less innocent and more and more dangerous. The gun owner who is head of the household should be aware of this. Maybe he does not realize that over time, his children grow up and become tall enough to reach the guns. The high schools change also. The schools which in his day were healthy learning centers, which had nary a shooting ever, are hot beds of drugs now. One of his boys is onto drugs, but he doesn't know it. The youngest son is socially challenged, is bullied in school and is a walking cauldron of hatred. His daughter has fallen under the influence of a good-for-nothing and dangerous Svengali. Whether he likes it or not, his household is inextricably connected with a world he doesn't see. So, what right does he have to be so sure about the safety of his guns?

The cases of mishaps by guns in the home abound. The story repeats time and again. Sarah Brady tells a chilling story along these lines and reveals the reason she became an activist against handguns. It was not because of the shooting in 1981in the nation's capital when President Reagan and his Press Secretary Jim Brady, Sarah's husband, were shot. People assume that this personal tragedy made her a crusader against the handgun. But, actually, that was not what did it.

It happens that months after the shooting, while visiting Jim's hometown in Illinois on vacation, an incident occurred that chilled her soul with fear.

They were waiting to go to the swimming pool of some friends, when she saw her six-year old son walking around with a handgun, pointing it at things, pretending to shoot at them. The gun belonged to one of their friends. She assumed it was a toy gun, but even so she did not like what she saw. Then she discovered that the gun was not a toy, that it was real and that it was fully loaded. That did it.

In order to have an idea of how often teenagers get hold of guns and go out on killing sprees, I queried Google about school shootings. The number of such shootings was staggering, so I limited them to the last two years, 2013 and 2014.

To be sure, it is possible that some of the shootings, even when committed by teenagers in high schools, may not involve guns taken from home. In some cases, the teenagers could have gotten the weapons in the black market. In the tables that follow I have left out the details of the shootings such as: the type of weapon used, the names or number of people killed or wounded and whether the assailant is in jail or committed suicide. The reader can get these details from the following link: **http://en.wikipedia. org/wiki/List_of_school_shootings_in_the_United_States**

Go to the above link and click on the case number given in brackets for full details.

SCHOOL SHOOTINGS 2013

DATE	PLACE	ASSAILANT
Jan. 10	Taft Union High School Taft, California	Brian Oliver, 16
Jan. 15	Stevens Inst. Bus. & Art St. Louis, Mo	Sean Johnson, student
Jan. 15	Hazard Community Tech Col Hazard, KY	Dalton Lee, 21
Jan. 31	Price Middle School Atlanta, Ga	Gunman, a student
Mar. 21	Davidson Middle School Southgate, Michigan	Tyler Nichols, 13
Apr. 16	Temple, TX.	Student suicide
Apr. 29	La Salle High School Cincinnati, Ohio	Joe Poynter, student
June 7	Santa Monica College Santa Monica, Ca	John Zawahri,

Aug. 20	Ronal McNair Learning Center Decatur, Ga	Michael Brandon Hill, 20
Aug. 30	Carver High School Winston-Salem, NC	Student, 18
Sept. 28	Gray New Gloucester High School Gary, Maine	Gaige McGue, 19
Oct. 15	Lanier High School Austin, TX	No Name, 17 Committed suicide
Oct. 21	Sparks Middle School Sparks, Nevada	Jose Reyes, 12
Dec. 13	Arapahoe High School Centennial, Colorado	Karl Pierson, 18
Dec. 19	Edison High School Fresno, California	Four teens

SCHOOL SHOOTINGS 2014

Jan. 9	Liberty Tech Magnet High School –Jackson, TN	Student, no age
Jan. 17	Delaware Valley Charter School –Philadelphia, Pa	Raisheem Rochwell, 17
Jan. 24	South Carolina State U Orangeburg, SC	Student, 19
Jan. 27	Rebound High School Carbondale, Illinois	Student, 18
Feb. 8	Bend High School Bend, Oregon	Zachary Leyes, 18
Feb. 10	Salisbury High School Salisbury, NC	Student, 17
May 23	UCLA Santa Bárbara Isla Vista, California	Elliot Rodger, 22
June 5	Seattle Pacific University Seattle, Washington	Aaron Ybarra, 26
June 10	Reynolds High School Troutdale, Oregon	Jared Padgett, 15
Sept. 10	Greenwood Lakes Middle School –Lake Mary, FL	Student, 14

Straw Purchases.

These are of two kinds: legal and illegal. The legal instances involve the purchase of ordinary objects, usually not weapons. For example, you purchase a car for someone whom you trust, but who cannot buy a car himself because of bad credit; or you buy groceries for senior citizens who can't get around well. The illegal cases involve guns, usually buying a gun for a minor, or a felon, or a person known to be mentally unstable. The seller involved in these transactions is also culpable if he sells weapons to a party knowing that the weapon is destined to a third party forbidden by law from buying the weapon.

Guns are not objects that should be gifted, as electric razors or cameras. Nor should they be lent, as brooms or vacuum cleaners. Nor should they be sold as discarded items in a garage sale. The gun owner should always be responsible for whatever use his gun is put to. If he sells it clandestinely or lends it, he is responsible for whatever purpose his gun buyer or borrower uses it.

I cite two recent cases here. The first concerns Dawn Nguyen, 25, who was sentenced in September 2014 to eight years in federal prison for buying a gun that was used to kill two New York firefighters. The second involves a Florida gun dealer, Lock N Load, for selling a gun that was used in a double homicide.

The Nguyen Case. The eight-year sentence of Ms. Nguyen may seem harsh. Some say that the courts are trying to use her case as an example to highlight the seriousness of the crime. Here are the particulars. She bought the gun for William Spengler, 61, a felon who spent 19 years in prison for bludgeoning to death his grandmother. Then, on December 24, 2012, Spengler set his home on fire to lure firefighters to his home in Webster, N.Y. and used the gun to kill two firefighters and wound two others. He ended it all by murdering his sister and killing himself.

Ms. Nguyen admitted that she knew Spengler was a dangerous felon. She also admitted to knowing that she had heard him threaten to kill his sister. But she did not know that Spengler had murdered his grandmother and did not take his threats to kill his sister seriously.

The Lock N Load Case. Unlike the above case in which the culpability applied strictly to two individuals and not to a business, this case does involve a business, a gun dealer in Oldsmar, Florida.

The Brady Center to Prevent Gun Violence is suing Lock N Load as part of a campaign against irresponsible so-called "bad Apple" gun dealers. The link to this case is http://www.bradycampaign.org/press-room/brady-center-sues-florida-gun-dealer-lock-n-load-for-selling-straw-purchased-gun-used-in. I quote:

"According to the lawsuit, Benjamin Bishop of Oldsmar, Florida obtained a shotgun from Lock N Load through a straw purchase carried out by a friend in 2012. Bishop, who suffers from schizophrenia and had a history of drug abuse, attempted to buy the shotgun but was denied because he had a criminal record. The lawsuit alleges that the dealer later sold the gun to Bishop's friend when the two teens returned to the store, and that Bishop returned a third time and was sold ammunition, despite the store's knowledge of his criminal record. In 2012, Bishop used the shotgun and ammunition to kill his mother Imari Shibata and her boyfriend Kelley Allen.

"The lawsuit alleges that Lock N Load failed to take reasonable steps to determine whether Bishop's friend was the actual purchaser of the shotgun, and that it was foreseeable that providing a gun to a straw purchaser, and ammunition to a prohibited purchaser, was likely to lead to death or injury."

These cases raise an interesting question about the very concept of "responsibility." What is its precise meaning anyway? In my opinion responsibility requires us to anticipate the worst scenarios and to take measures to prevent them; it compels us to act in the best interest of all, especially of others. If you recognize certain actions that could lead to a crime, then avoid them, prevent them. But if the worst does come to pass, you should not wash your hands off the affair by claiming that you did nothing criminal yourself because you did not pull the trigger. Own up to your part of the process.

People who act irresponsibly tend to make excuses for themselves and think that because they do not have a motive to kill someone, because they do not even know the potential victim it is okay to help a friend by giving him a gun to kill a stranger. Abetting may be a lesser crime, but you still share the blame. This is a pernicious attitude that can only be stamped out by punishing it harshly.

Unfortunately, some of the extreme cases of gun irresponsibility are not illegal, at least not yet. This is the case with Ghost Guns.

Ghost Guns. These are guns whose parts can be bought by mail and assembled at home. They are called "ghost guns" because there is no control on the purchase of these guns and, thus, they leave no trace. They have no serial number, there is no background check; there is no waiting period; they are a criminal's delight.

Supposedly, the receiver of these guns –which is the part where the serial number is written –cannot be bought without a serial number. However, people can make their own. It is not an insuperable impediment. For practical purposes, the guns can be made without trace. By this method you can make AR-15 and AK-47 type weapons. Who needs a gun store or a gun dealer when you can make your own. One such weapon was made and used in the killing spree of Santa Monica of June 2013, when John Zawahri went on a killing spree.

In the next chapter I deal with more instances of irresponsibility as they pertain to the use of objects other than guns.

CHAPTER 13

Social Irresponsibility

● ● ●

EACH DAY PEOPLE FIND NEW ways to use technology irresponsibly. Our new marvelous gadgets facilitate our lives, but they come full of vulnerabilities. Technology has brought us hacking; identity theft; drones that invade our privacy and interfere with aviation; lasers aimed at the cockpit of commercial planes to blind pilots; dangers on the road due to texting; telemarketing that invades your privacy; pressure cookers to make bombs; and, of all things, 3D printers that are capable of making all sorts of things, including guns. You can make your own gun hooch at home, even AK47s with a 3D printer.

Fortunately, these printers cannot be bought outright. They are acquired through lease agreements. But once you have one, you just enter the design specifications of an object, you put in the plastic (the building material) and lo and behold, the printer materializes the object in full solid three dimensions. Who would have thought that one could manufacture things at home with a 3D-Printer and guns of all things? This new technology throws gun controls out the window because anyone can now make his own weapon and sell it. To add insult to injury, the weapons can be passed through airport and X-ray devices because they are non-metallic. It is a killer's dream, the policeman's nightmare.

This is the brave new world we are in. The company which started it all was Solid Concepts Inc., based in Valencia, CA. Since then it has changed its name to **Stratsys.** This is a custom manufacturing company engaged in engineering, manufacturing, production, and prototyping.

They make business products, aerospace, unmanned systems, medical equipment, foundry cast patterns, industrial equipment and design, and transportation parts. But I must emphasize that this is an honest, responsible company. It was not their intent to have people make their guns at home. Their technology was perverted to nefarious uses and it didn't take long.

Enter Cody Rutledge Wilson (born January 31, 1988), a young, very creative and irresponsible tinkerer, who has been called a "crypto-anarchist" for his gun-rights views. He is the founder and director of Defense Distributed, a non-profit organization that develops and publishes gun designs, also known as "wiki-weapons." He is also a co-founder of **Dark Wallet**, a bitcoin storage outfit that permits money exchanges through the Internet that cannot be tracked. Pedophiles, drug dealers and prostitution rings would be interested in the services of his company as well as anybody who uses the "dark web" –the untraceable Internet of the demimonde.

Wilson's company, Defense Distributed, made a big splash in 2013 when it disseminated through the Internet the plans to make a pistol called "The Liberator" with a 3D printer. *Wired Magazine's* "Danger Room" named him one of the "15 most dangerous people in the world" in 2012. Then in January, 2015, *Wired* named Wilson the fifth most dangerous person on the Internet.

When Stratsys learned of Wilson's plans to make guns, it threatened legal action and demanded the return of its 3D printer. Stratsys then cancelled its lease and confiscated the printer. Wikipedia, which is my source on all this, has ample information on the doings and comings and goings of Wilson.

How do we cope with the maverick, dangerous individuals who use new technologies irresponsibly? The 3D printer is only one of many modern devices that are used for purposes for which they were not intended. It behooves us to analyze these malicious practices and note their common characteristics. Typically, the majority of users are law-abiding, responsible individuals. The litterbugs and evil users are few. The situation is reminiscent of the asymmetry of guns in America, in that it echoes the argument from responsible gun owners who decry the fact that irresponsible people give gun owners a bad name when they use the guns to kill people. The responsible gun owners point out that they and thousands of others own guns and do not go around killing people. This same situation plays again with smart phones, lasers, drones and the Internet. It is only a few miscreants who ruin it for all. Let us set up a framework for analyzing this phenomenon.

A Probabilistic Model. Suppose a device is used responsibly 95% of the time and 5% it is not. Further, when it is used irresponsibly, the perpetrator can be traced and caught in only one percent of the instances. In four percent of the abuses he gets away. From these considerations I construct the following table. All figures are hypothetical.

	R	R'	Total
T	0	1	1
T'	95	4	99
total	95	5	100

R = Used responsibly   R' = Used irresponsibly

T = User was traced   T' = User was not traced

Two conditional probabilities concern us here. They are confusing because they seem so similar, but they are the difference of night and day and it behooves us to keep them straight. The first is:

$$P(R'/T') = 4/99 = 0.0404$$

In 99 percent of the cases that the device is used it cannot be traced. Fortunately, most people use it responsibly (95 out of the 99). But a few of these (4 out of 99) do not use it responsibly. This probability basically quantifies the number of bad apples in the community and thank goodness it is low. The second probability flips the variables of interest and focuses from a different perspective. This probability is:

$$P(T'/R') = 4/5 = 80\%$$

This says that out of the 5 who use the device irresponsibly, 4 will not be caught because they can't be traced. This is the probability that would be of interest to an irresponsible person. He would ask himself: what are my chances of getting away with it if I misuse it? The high probability of not getting caught invites mischief. And this is a good part of our problem.

The majority of people are not interested in mischief, even if they knew that they would not get caught. They are not litterbugs; they have a social conscience; they care for the common weal. But the few who are prone to mischief can cause considerable damage. For these people it is all play at little cost to them. There is no penalty for malfeasance because they figure they won't get caught. What are we to do about this situation? Where is the Achilles Heel of the perpetrators?

It is difficult to generalize with so many gadgets around. We have to analyze the situations case by case, gadget by gadget. But, in general, confiscation or banning the devices is not an optimal solution. It would be unfair to deprive the majority of responsible users for the irresponsible actions of the few. We have to learn to live and cope with new technology.

Detection of misuse is the key in many situations. Detection can be in and of itself a deterrent. But detection may require the assistance of new countervailing technology. If this technology does not exist, it would need to be invented and designed specifically for that gadget. Let's consider specific devices to see appropriate responses.

Telemarketing. This is the practice where the telephone is abused for advertising purposes. One solution was to create a registry that would make your phone number off limits to the telemarketers. You submit your request for a cease-and-desist order and supposedly the telemarketers have to respect it and not call you anymore. Another solution was more technological and more effective. The telephone company came up with a device known as "caller ID" which identifies the caller. A voice recording announces and identifies the caller. If you know the caller, you pick up the receiver; but if the voice identifies the caller as "unavailable" or "anonymous" you just don't answer the phone. Let them leave you a message.

Drones. These are basically fancy toys. Most people use them for amusement, but Amazon wants to use them to make deliveries.

Photographers often use them to get aerial pictures. The abuses range from peeping toms to terrorism. When used irresponsibly around airports, they could bring down a commercial airline. They could also be used to invade the White House.

Drones are easy to control. First, require all drones to have a serial number. Second, require them to be registered. Third, define the permissible limits of use, banning them from the vicinity of airports, around the White House or other public buildings. Fourth, the devices will be picked off from the sky or shot down. The owner could easily be traced by the serial number and the owner will be fined and prosecuted. In this case, the contingency table would now be as follows,

	R	R'	Total
T	0	4	4
T'	95	1	96
total	95	5	100

R = Used responsibly   R' = Used irresponsibly
T = User was traced   T' = User was not traced

Now, four out of the five irresponsible users get caught. Only one out of five gets away. The probability of acting irresponsible given that you cannot be traced is even lower than before: $P(R'/T') = 1/96 = 0.01$. Further, the probability of getting caught given that you act irresponsibly is: $P(T/R') = 4/5 = 0.80$. The tables have been turned on the perps. Safety for malfeasance has been significantly reduced because now the probability that you will not get caught given that you act irresponsibly is much lower: $P(T'/R') = 1/5 = 0.20$.

Laser beams. These are the high-powered laser flashes that can reach long distances. Astronomy aficionados use them to point to the stars for students learning the constellations. But others use them to aim at the eyes of a pilot in a commercial airline. Big, dangerous fun! Because these devices are cheap and readily available and because as of now there is no technological antidote against them, they are difficult to control.

The relevant question here is: are they worth it? Since there is no compelling use for them, and since they have the potential of causing great harm, this calls for a techno-economic solution. First, ban outright the current cheap toys. Second, come up with an alternative laser with a transmitter that emits an identifying signal when in use. This newer model would cost more and would tend to price out the frivolous users. Only universities and serious astronomers would find them useful. They should not be the abundant cheap toys that they are now.

What to do with the remaining cheap lasers already out in the hands of troublemakers? One may argue that, as with guns, buy-backs would not be very effective because only the responsible owners would turn in their lasers, leaving only the "bad guys" in possession of the banned cheap lasers.

Actually, the buy-back program is defensible on two grounds. First, it is fair because it compensates the responsible users for possessing something which is now illegal, but which they never abused. Second, it is good advertising for the new law; it helps condemn the old lasers for what they are: harmful, undesirable and illegal toys. It also helps to propagate the right message: get rid of them. The buy-back would be complemented with laws that punish the possession of the old lasers with stiff penalties. We could also reward people for information leading to the capture of such lasers. Last, perhaps putting cameras throughout the city, especially around airports, could help locate the source of the laser beam and help win the war against their mischievous use. If successful, in time the contingency table would be ideal and would look as follows. The T' row would be all zero.

R = Used responsibly   R' = Used irresponsibly
T = User was traced   T' = User was not traced

	R	R'	Total
T	95	5	100
T'	0	0	0
total	95	5	100

The story here is that the cameras, the public vigilance and their reporting have managed to achieve 100% detection, $P(T) = 1$. Even more significant is the fact that the probability that troublemakers will be caught is also a certainty since: $P(T/R') = 5/5 = 1$.

It is worth noting that this has not changed the character of the people. It is still the case that 5 percent of the people are irresponsible.

Such is human nature and we can't change it. But the criminals have been rendered ineffective. They can no longer get away with breaking the law. Their crime does not pay.

3D Printers. No obvious solution is yet available here. Criminals now have the plans and the manual for making the guns. What they don't have is the printer with which to make them. So far Stratys has managed to control that very tightly. As with many other ordinary gadgets and utensils that can be used by terrorists (pressure cookers as in the Boston bombers, fertilizer as in the Oklahoma Federal building bomber, commercial planes as in September 11, and now 3D printers), the evil genie is out and we have to control the potential misuse of these tools and materials.

CHAPTER 14

Gun Registration

● ● ●

CONGRESS HAS PUT SO MANY restrictions on the ATF, the Bureau of Alcohol, Tobacco and Firearms, that the agency is hampered and impeded from tracing a gun's history or exercising other forms of gun controls. The situation is a nightmare.

"A gun trace that should normally take minutes instead takes days, wasting precious time and millions of taxpayers' dollars." (Editorial Board, the Los Angeles Times, September 8, 2016).

Also, according to the Law Center to Prevent Gun Violence this is the situation in the country today:

"There is no comprehensive national system of gun registration. In fact, federal law prohibits the use of the National Instant Criminal Background Check System (NICS) to create any system of registration of firearms or firearm owners.[5"] A limited system of federal firearms registration was created by the National Firearms Act, 26 U.S.C. § 5801 *et seq.* The National Firearms Act ("NFA") was enacted in 1934 to impose an excise tax and registration requirements on a narrow category of firearms, including machine guns, short-barreled shotguns or rifles, and silencers, and these weapons must also be registered under the NFA.[6] With its provisions effectively limited to pre-ban machine guns and transfers of short-barreled rifles and shotguns that are specifically authorized by the Attorney General, the registration system created by the National Firearms Act falls far short of a comprehensive registration system. http://smartgunlaws.org/registration-of-firearms-policy-summary/

As if this were not enough, there is also a big loophole that enables some gun buyers to buy guns legally but under the radar, avoiding any sort of registration or records. Here is how that occurs. At present, all gun dealers are required to get a license from the ATF. They are required to keep records and make them available to the ATF when requested. However, private dealers can get around this on the ground that they are hobbyists, selling their collections person-to-person as in a garage sale. These hobbyists are not required to have a license. The guns they sell are just like used toaster ovens. They require no background checks from buyers. They maintain no records. Why should a criminal needing a gun bother with a licensed dealer? For the criminal it isn't even necessary to steal a gun. The "gun show loophole," as this setup is called, is his best ticket. One would think that it should be easy to close this loophole. President Obama has certainly tried and failed because, you must remember, this is the United States and in this country the power to control guns is in the hands of the gun lobbies. This has to change. It is such a no-brainer. This loophole nullifies the controls imposed upon the gun dealers.

Cars, boats, motorcycles and real estate property have to be registered. So why not guns? Guns have managed to be exempted. The lack of registration plus the loopholes give gun buyers the advantage of cover and anonymity. It makes it harder to trace to the responsible party when someone has been killed.

How have we gotten into this situation? The short answer is that the gun lobby doesn't want gun registration. They fear it is a slippery slope to gun confiscation. They block it on the grounds that once your gun is registered, then the Federal Government knows where to come for your gun.

Assuming they were right to be paranoid, that the Feds really wanted to take their guns, do they really believe that the lack of registration would stop them? This and other arguments against gun registration are nonsensical. Another such is the claim that registration does not stop crime. Who claimed that? It may not stop crime, but it shouldn't abet crime by making it so easy to buy guns under the radar as it does now.

The issue of gun registration is so weird that it invites whimsy. It happens that gun registration is in conflict with the Fifth Amendment and this conflict is downright farcical. In a famous case, **Haynes vs U.S**. (1968), a convicted felon, Miles Edward Haynes, came up with a clever defense for not registering. He claimed he could not be charged for failing to register a gun he owned on the grounds that as a convicted felon who was banned from owning a gun, he would be incriminating himself if he tried to register it. The case went to the Supreme Court of the United States and Haynes won. The verdict was eight to one in his favor. Chief Justice Earl Warren cast the dissenting vote.

The real crime here is that Haynes was able to get a gun. If the loopholes did not exist, he would have had to borrow or steal the gun. If the gun was registered, then its rightful owner passed it on to Haynes by either lending it to Haynes or losing it to Haynes. If Haynes stole it, he could be tried for stealing and, also, for possessing a gun as a felon. Forget about prosecuting him for failure to register the gun. The law has enough on him as it is.

Finally, some may argue that people will always find a way to sell their guns person-to-person and nobody will know about it. This is not necessarily true. Actually, whether they can get away with this or not depends on how effective our gun registration is. If registration is no joke; if it has a national data base that traces guns in minutes, then this fosters respect for the law. Among other things, it protects the individual gun seller. If a gun is registered in your name and you are responsible for its use or misuse, it behooves you to be protected when you do sell it. You don't want your gun to be involved in a murder that is traceable to you. For protection, you could display it in your garage sale, but the actual transfer will have to be effected at a registered dealer's establishment with all the requisites of the law thereto appertaining. Registration helps you unload a hot potato.

CHAPTER 15

Gun Rights and the Second Amendment

● ● ●

GUN LOVERS ARE AT THE pinnacle of their power in America; they have the laws protecting their rights and the political clout in Washington. And yet they sit uneasy, acting as if gun confiscation was around the corner. At the slightest hint of any adjustment in gun laws, the gun advocates see the slippery slope that leads to gun confiscation and they sound off their Chicken Little cry: "They're coming for our guns."

The Second Amendment is their protective mantle. Some would say this old document is irrelevant to our time with its talk about militias in colonial America. But actually (and many people may have forgotten this) it has been recently brought up to date. In two recent cases (2008) and (2010), the Supreme Court of the United States ruled that the arcane ambiguous language from antiquity applied to our world today. But the devil is in the details. What guns? Where? By these decisions the amendment got a fresh new coating that specifically covers handguns.

In **District of Columbia v. Heller** (2008) the Court ruled that the people in the District of Columbia had the right to possess a firearm for traditionally lawful purposes, such as self-defense. Specifically, the ordinary people living in the nation's capital (and not just defensive militias) could have their guns for self-defense. This immediately raised the question: What about the rest of Americans –those who live outside the capital in the fifty states? Would this right also extend to them? This issue was affirmed two years later in the next ruling.

In **McDonald v. Chicago** (2010) the Supreme Court affirmed for the first time the right of gun ownership for self-defense to all Americans in the 21st Century, not only in the District of Columbia, but everywhere else as well.

One would think that this should have put all those fears of gun confiscation to rest. The ruling gave gun lovers a clear victory, although not a resounding one, the vote was 5 to 4. I have no problem with this decision, as long as this right applies specifically to handguns. But there is the rub. Many questions remain as to **what** guns, **who** uses them **where** and **when.** The entire matter is not clear yet. Even now there are situations where this right is abridged and denied. It is not absolute. Guns are being confiscated on a daily basis throughout America without raising any hackles. This takes place, for example, at airports where regardless of the sex, age or race of the gun owner, his right to "bear arms" is denied. His weapons are confiscated. This also takes place in prisons, in hospitals and in courthouses. The Second Amendment does not apply everywhere. But there are exceptions. Some states are bucking this current and going in the opposite direction. They are broadening the scope of the Second Amendment by explicitly designating areas where guns can be taken. They are giving their blessings for people to carry guns into churches and college campuses.

There is a jockeying for power and say-so as to who carries what guns where. Some people are denied the right to own guns, others lose that right. For example, minors, deranged individuals and convicted felons may not own guns. Wherever they happen to be, guns can be confiscated from them. This is all perfectly legal. Even the NRA does not object to these exceptions. As time passes even more restrictions come into mind. But also more allowances for shooting guns are granted. There are people who take their children to firing ranges and educate them on the use of guns. On the restrictive side, there are cases coming through the lower courts questioning whether domestic abusers, men who are violent and who threaten their wives, should be banned from owning guns.

Civilization develops little by little, at a snail's pace. In democracies it is particularly slow. It takes decades, much thinking, much maturing and dying before laws are amended to reflect the tenor of a wise and just society. There is still more, much more to be done about guns. And this may be at the bottom of what gun lovers fear. They know that in the end we will get it right and clarify the limits and exceptions to the Second Amendment.

Weapons Other than Handguns. This is where the fight looms now. More and more people and institutions are expressing their dislike and discontent about rapid-fire rifles. The New York Times would ban them outright. I think we can compromise on that by allowing people to own them, but under strict controls. These weapons would have to be registered; people could not keep them at home; and they could be fired only at the firing range. I hope a brave congressman in the near future will come up with such a bill and I hope that by then the political climate would have changed enough so that the bill would have a good chance of being passed. It shouldn't be difficult to make a case for this.

What arguments can be made in favor of the civilian population owning these weapons and keeping them at home? I can think of only a few and they are not very compelling.

The First Argument: convenience. The gun owners derive utility – that is, joy, pride, titillation, jollies –from having their guns at home. It is natural to want all your possessions to be near you; you want your statues, your craftworks, your art pieces, your furniture, your tools, your clothing and your belongings at home near you. So, why not your AK-47s as well?

Big difference! These guns are too deadly for society to risk leaving them loose in the hands of potential killers. It takes only a few killers to wreak havoc and cause great damage. Why make it easy for them? Why give them so much convenience? By not allowing these guns in the homes we can thwart massacres.

Yes, but are we not penalizing the majority of gun owners who are not killers by doing that? Why inconvenience the majority? The answer is that the cost of inconvenience is miniscule in comparison to the benefit gained from preventing massacres. The logistical inconvenience is not worth the expected cost of innocent lives lost.

In addition, there is this: the guns cannot be fired for pleasure or practice within city limits. There are city ordinances against that. So, the guns have to be taken out to firing ranges or to places in the boonies to be fired. What then do the gun owners have to gain by keeping guns at home where they cannot fire them to begin with?

A Second Argument: Sports. To a clastomaniac (someone with a penchant for destruction) these weapons are fun, a dream toy. The man or woman that goes for these weapons loves their destructive power. He or she loves to blow to smithereens glass bottles, clay pigeons and mow down wheat stubbles in a field with bullets. He is a closet warrior, playing war games, dreaming of the day when the Olympic Committee will create a new competition with these weapons. Fine. Everyone to their own taste. As long as these weapons are kept under strict supervision so that they are used only for sport they can keep them, but only at the firing range. The cost of inconvenience is outweighed by the benefit accrued from the prevention of mayhem.

A Third Argument: Self-Defense. They already have handguns at home for self-defense. We have already covered that. The Supreme Court rulings have upheld that right. I got no problem with that. We are talking about rapid-fire rifles here, AK-47s and the like, not handguns.

How much firepower do you need for self-defense? These guns exceed all reasonable bounds. The owner of such guns must relish the sense of invincibility that these weapons afford with their awesome killing power; he must take comfort in knowing that he can outgun anybody, that he can handle not just one home-invader, but three, or four, or a whole squad of them. Why, he is prepared for a little war in his home.

But is self-defense a carte blanche to turn your home into an arsenal? Why not a tank in your garage and rocket launchers also? What governs how much firepower is necessary for normal and credible self-defense?

That depends, of course, on the threats you face. So we should ask: Are American homes besieged? Who is clamoring for so much firepower in the name of self-defense? Here are some examples of the types of individuals who come to mind to justify these guns for this degree of self-defense.

The gangster, the mafia capo. Anyone who has lived by the gun has reason to believe that he will die by the gun. He should live in a fortress, not a home. An underworld figure would definitely need these guns. Of course, in his case the point is moot because the gangster wouldn't be asking the support of the laws to ensure his defense. He would have an arsenal, legal or not.

The psychologically insecure. You don't have to be in real danger and you don't need to have real enemies to claim self-defense and arm for war. It suffices that *you think* you are in danger. You could be an ordinary Joe who thinks the world is at war with you. If you imagine many enemies and you fear that they are coming after you, of course you would feel a need for great firepower. The question is: should you be able to use your paranoia as grounds for self-defense?

The proto-anarchist. This guy marches to a revolutionary drummer. He has scores to settle with his culture, with society, with the political system or with some racial or ethnic segments of the population. He could be a malcontent, someone who thinks the world has robbed him of much and he wants to be ready for that day of reckoning when he can even the score. He smells war in the air in every season of the year.

All the above individuals would say, if asked, that they need the rapid-fire weapons for self-defense. Self-defense is the catch-all pretext. But the invocation of self-defense manifests only the existence of some fear. It is these fears that we need to question before granting the guns for self-defense. The trouble is that there are fears and fears and we never ask: what fear? We never demand that people spell out the specific fear that, supposedly, only an AK-47s can allay.

Well, I have my own fears. I fear unnecessary killings and carnage from these guns. I fear that we are going to the dogs with firepower gone amok. We have, in effect, a war of fears. This war of fears has up to now accommodated only one side: the side that feels that only guns can allay their fears –the more firepower the better. So I ask: what is the hierarchy in the game of fears? Which and whose fears trump what fears? By couching their fears in the name of self-defense the public clamors for faster and more lethal weapons and the gun manufacturers and the NRA all too conveniently rush to accommodate them. Gun dealers pander to unjustified self-defense arguments. What about my fears, my fear of turning our country into a Wild West?

Self-Defense versus Self-Protection. It is easy to confuse self-defense with self-protection. They are not the same thing. Consider this example. A woman discovers that she made a mistake with her live-in male companion. He drinks; he is a bully; he abuses her; he has roughed her up already and has threatened to kill her if she reports him or tries to fight back. He has a gun and is comfortable with it. She has never held a gun in her life and is not comfortable with guns. Unquestionably, she needs protection. But does a gun afford protection in her case? Are there better alternatives?

Self- protection would counsel her to avoid a shootout and to get out of there. Self-defense would prod her to stay in place, to get ready for the shootout, hoping she could shoot her bully first.

For me, self-defense –the gun in this case –is a bad idea. The woman should vanish to a safe haven away from him. Then, from her safe hiding she should report him. All she wants is to be rid of him. Let time cool things. In the end she would be rid of him and she would survive. That's the way to go.

What to do about rapid-fire rifles? Perhaps these weapons have proliferated in the belief that the American people do not object. Their silence is taken as acquiescence. Perhaps, also, people are under the impression that these weapons are covered by The Second Amendment and that, whether we like it or not, we are stuck with these weapons forever. They are an inseparable part of our culture. Guns R Us. That's America.

They are not covered by the Second Amendment. Their days should be numbered. The silence about them has been broken. The first critical outcry against these weapons was made by **The New York Times** in a rare front-cover editorial (December 4, 2015) where it decried the easy accessibility of these weapons and said enough! It's time we ban these weapons from the homes once and for all. These weapons are monstrous.

The case for these weapons is trivial and comes to logistical convenience, sport, or questionable self-defense. The case against them is grave and involves the protection of human lives and the validation of the rights for liberty and the pursuit of happiness aspired for and proclaimed by the founding founders in the Bill of Rights. So many innocent lives have been lost due to the accommodation of these monstrous weapons in our midst. Our land has been turned into a war zone. And all for no good reason. We have pandered to the convenience of gun lovers, to their obsession with their sport requiring faster, more efficient killing machines, and to their unjustified claims for self-defense.

Would a law banning these weapons from the homes violate the Second Amendment? If so, show me where. Where does the Second Amendment say that you can have such weapons at home? Those weapons weren't even dreamed of at the time the Second Amendment was written. And the purpose for which they have been used, so callously and against innocent people, was not contemplated by the framers of the amendment. You would have to stretch the intent of the founding fathers and warp their words to come up with a justification for the killings that these weapons have wrought. As Chief Justice Warren Burger aptly put it, a "fraud" has been perpetrated on the American people in the name of the Second Amendment.

If the purpose for guns in the homes is self-defense, then handguns should do. If the purpose is shooting the rapid-fire rifles for sport, then this should be done at the firing range. By allowing Americans to keep a handgun at home and by allowing them to own an AK-47 and even fire it (at the firing range), the Second Amendment has been adhered to and complied with. Let us now note how such a ban would have served us.

Recent Massacres. Gun lovers often criticize gun laws for their ineffectiveness. They love to point out that background checks and other statutes would not have prevented certain killings. For example, in some instances the killer did not buy the gun, he stole it. Therefore, crossing all the t's and dotting all the i's on gun sale is an exercise in futility. Or, the killer bought the gun legally; he was outwardly hale and upright at the time he bought it. But he snapped later and went on a killing spree. That is not the fault of the background checks. Therefore, gun laws don't work.

Well, this law would have worked. The law I propose would ban rapid-fire weapons from the home. In addition, the possession and firing of these weapons would put them on guard that they have a 75% chance of having their home searched randomly. The police and the FBI would have grounds to get a search warrant from a judge, which they could exercise at any time. They could search for other weapons and gun paraphernalia to determine what they are dealing with. Here is how this law would have prevented some of the recent massacres.

San Bernardino shooting (2015). The killers in this case were Farook and his wife. These killers raise interesting issues which compel us to reconsider the distinction between profiling and prudent regard for our suspicions. Normally, the comings and goings of people should be of no concern to the government. But it depends on who is doing the travelling and where they are going.

Here is Farook, a male in his 20s, making not one but two trips to Mecca; he marries a stranger, someone he met in Saudi Arabia on his trip, a Pakistani, Arab-speaking woman. Should this cause alarm? Twenty years ago it should not have. But since ISIS, since the attacks in Paris, since the recruitment of future jihadists over the Internet, it should have. Farook should have been on the FBI's watch. Then here is the clincher. All of a sudden, after his return from Mecca, this quiet and religious food inspector and his wife develop a love for AK-47s. They borrow a friend's weapons. They who wouldn't kill a fly are going to the firing range on a daily basis and shooting AK-47s as if they were training for war. That should have alarmed the FBI enough to get a warrant to inspect their home. If they had, look what they would have found: a baby amid pipe bombs in the making. We would have learned what we now know, but we would have learned it in time to foil their plots and schemes.

Sandy Hook Elementary School (2012). This case has the tragic overtones and undertones of the most ominous dark tales from Greek mythology. Here is a woman who lives alone with her unstable teen-age son, Adam Lanza. She keeps an arsenal of military-type weapons at home. No fishing or sports activities for them. Their big pastime is violent daydreaming which takes them to the firing range to give vent to their fantasies and shoot away. It is hard to place their life within an ordinary or normal framework. Their life conjures up only dark sinister scenarios. What was she thinking? What did she think she was doing?

Then one day Fate plays its hand with a comeuppance that any old soothsayer from the old world would have predicted. Adam's demons emerge, claiming, perhaps, that the guns are tired of shooting at targets, at bottles, at clay pigeons. They are clamoring for human blood, for children's blood, for women's blood and he tells his mother: "I'll start with you, Mom. You need to die." Then he dispatches her and proceeds to the elementary school to kill 26 people in all, mostly children.

The law in question would definitely have prevented this. Adam Lanza's mother could not have kept the arsenal of weapons she kept at home. Without those guns at home, Lanza would have had to use handguns. He would have killed his mother using the pistols and he would have had to limit himself to those weapons for the school. He would have killed considerably fewer people.

Aurora, Colorado (July 19, 2012). James Holmes opened fire in a movie theater, killing 12 and wounding 27 people. Holmes had been under psychiatric care. His psychiatrist, Dr. Lynne Fenton, suspected that he could be dangerous and reported to the university campus police that Holmes had made homicidal statements one month before the shooting. Remarkably, this was not acted upon.

Several other reports about his alarming condition have materialized, but as is often the case with retrospective accounts they are inconsequential; they are warnings, they are like the pile of charred match-sticks that point to the failed attempts to ignite a fire. For example, a graduate student was told two weeks before the shooting that he, Holmes himself, had dysphoric mania and was "bad news." Holmes warned this fellow to stay away from him. I will spare you the other belated reports because they serve only as titillating remembrances after the fact. But the doctor's report is different. That should have made a difference, particularly in light of the following chronology.

> May 22, Holmes buys a Glock 22 pistol at a gun shop in Aurora
> May 28, he buys a Remington 870 Express in Denver
> June 7, he buys a high-powered rifle
> A month before the killing, he buys 3000 rounds for the guns and 350 shells for the shotgun over the Internet.
> July 2, he places an order for a Blackhawk assault vest and two magazine holders.

Where is the war? Why should a graduate student be accumulating an arsenal? When the police first heard Dr. Fenton's warnings they should have cast a wide investigative net, covering all gun shops in the area and the Internet. Has this man bought any weapons? If he tries to, give us a call. He could have been caught.

Although he would have broken no law by all his purchases, you have to be blind not to see what was coming. There was ample justification for a search warrant to inspect his apartment and discover that he was up to no good.

Brutal Irony. As if the wanton killings weren't enough, there are also the flukes and unforeseen killings with these guns. Fate plays its nasty card so satanically sometimes, with an irony, so acrid that it scalds for a long time after you first learn of it. It is as if the gun itself was in control and used the shooter's body to consummate the kill.

In one case, one of the most decorated heroes of the Iraq War was killed in a firing range near Chalk Mountain, Texas, on February 2, 2013. The killing was unexpected, but it was no accident. Christopher Scott Kyle was the murder victim, the man whose autobiography *American Sniper* (2009) is well known to all Americans. The book was later made into a movie of the same name. Eddie Ray Routh, a former marine, opened fire at the firing range killing Kyle and a friend, Chad Littlefield. The killer, Routh, is now serving a life sentence.

The second case occurred on August 25, 2014 in a gun range called the "Arizona Last Stop." It is just as ironic as the first case and perhaps a little more bizarre. Charles Vacca was a 39-year-old instructor at the range. He had been teaching a 9-year-old girl to shoot an Uzi when something went terribly wrong. The girl shot and killed him. Her name has not been revealed. This was an accident.

I see these weapons as minions of death, fulfilling the purpose for which they were created, killing someone –although not necessarily an intended target, an enemy, a bad guy. Sometimes they manage to kill people who are by all counts the least likely to be killed by them, the expert shooters, the lord and masters of these weapons. Did the gun turn on the master? What would it have to say for itself if it could talk? I can just see the gun shrugging as smoke comes out of its nostril. All it can say for itself is: I told you I was dangerous.

CHAPTER 16

Police and Guns

● ● ●

THANKS TO CAMERAS AND SMART phones the whole country is now a witness to the shootings and killings by police. The nightly TV news has turned our living rooms into courtrooms and us, the people, into witnesses of possible police misconduct. The frequency of these incidents is staggering and prompts us to ask: has it always been like this? Are the cameras just now exposing what has been going on for years? The videos are visual indictments of the police which document the use of excessive force and capture times when dangerous situations were woefully mismanaged.

But, although we all look at the same videos, we do not draw the same conclusions. Black Americans, in particular, see rampant racism. The statistics would appear to buttress this charge, but actually it is a facile conclusion. The problem is more complex and involves other factors which are not given their due. I, personally, do not see as much racism as they do. I do not believe that the police are out to kill blacks –although, of course, for one reason or another they are doing so.

What, besides racism, is driving these shootings? The other factors are just as bad, and they are: police stupidity, police brutality, poor police training and police excitability in charged situations. Moreover, the wrongdoing pervades all levels –not only the cop on the scene, but his superiors, the ones who make policy, the ones who make the protocols, the ones who decide what tools are to be used in apprehending individuals, the ones who need to be doing the thinking, but are not.

Let's begin with the most egregious and most incredible case, which occurred when a 73-year-old insurance executive, Robert Bates, shot Eric Harris, on April 2, 2015 in Tulsa, Oklahoma. What does this have to do with the police? It happens that Bates loved to play cop on his time off and —because he was a big contributor to the police fund and because he was a friend of the sheriff —Bates was allowed to go on patrols with the police and was even given a gun and a Taser to boot. In one of these patrols, things went terribly awry. Bates mistook his gun for his Taser and, just like that, by a stupid amateurish mishandling of his weapons, he killed Eric Harris. This should not have happened. He should not have been going on patrol in the first place and certainly not armed. How could he mistake a Taser for a gun? How could the sheriff allow this?

Bates was white, Harris was black. Yet, racism was not an issue here. Instead, this case exemplifies the other non-racial factors that I alluded to above: police stupidity, unprofessional conduct and mismanagement.

What is astounding is that this is not the only case of police firings resulting in deaths. There are 54 more in recent history. For a detailed summary of these, visit the following Washington Post link: (click the mouse while pressing the control key)

https://www.washingtonpost.com/news/post-nation/wp/2015/
04/13/tulsa-case-adds-to-count-of-police-officers-charged-in-
fatal-on-duty-shootings/?tid=a_inl&utm_term=.19f92c612cf2

On this link you will find names, dates, places and circumstances. And there is more. Since this article appeared other killings by police have occurred with seismic consequences that have erupted into riots and violent protests across the land.

Typically, in all these fatal situations the adrenalin rushes and emotions seethe to the point of combustion. Fear, anger and frustration percolate in a boiling cauldron. Reason, caution and emotional control, which should be the governing forces, are instead overwhelmed by knee-jerk responses. Then the gun adds the last fatal straw, exacerbating the precarious circumstances by turning bad decisions into fast-paced irreversible tragedies. The cop, who should anticipate where things are headed and should strive to cool them, instead gets caught in the maelstrom of emotions. The gun then overwhelms the policeman by exerting its own will and manipulating the trigger.

There is no excuse for a policeman to shoot at a fleeing unarmed man in the back. What is the danger? Is it that the fleeing man will get away? If so, if apprehending him is that important, why not shoot at the legs? Why don't they train the policemen to do this? Why do things get so out of control? To my mind, the policeman's mission is not clear. His priorities are not specific enough.

Policemen are empowered with an awesome right, the right to kill. This right is fraught with dangers and should not be exercised lightly. It should have more checks and balances. The videos show that the policemen are not careful enough. This right has not always been exercised professionally and with due care, but wantonly. Here are some reflections on this issue.

1) I do not advocate eliminating the policeman's empowerment to kill, certainly not in our day and age when it is indispensable for the policeman on the beat.
2) But it should be applied only in cases where human lives are in clear and imminent danger.
3) Unfortunately, the stricture "clear and imminent danger" is subjective. The word "danger," in particular, always appears different with 20-20 hindsight.
   We should strive to take out the subjectivity as much as possible and specify concrete conditions when it should and should not apply. The videos can help here.
4) For example, shoot to kill should never apply when the fleeing suspect is not armed and the policeman has to shoot him in the

back. Observance of this rule would have eliminated a lot of cases.

5) The right to kill is corrupting; it goes to the policeman's head and it slips out of his fingers. Many men cannot handle it. When provoked and harassed a cop can lose it. If he is disobeyed and scorned; if his authority is challenged, if the suspect tries to flee, the policeman may resort to the gun. Perhaps he doesn't intend to kill; perhaps he merely wants to scare. What he must realize is that he is playing with fire that could burn him.

6) In the days before the ubiquitous cameras, the cop could disregard the fear of getting burned because he had the advantage of secrecy, which enabled him to err, even to abuse his power without fear of being caught. If he killed someone by mistake, it was his word against that of a dead perp. He could always rationalize his actions to ease his conscience, or he could concoct a justifiable scenario after the fact.

7) The cameras have diminished this protection. The cop has to worry not only about the eyes of his own conscience, but the eyes of the world which may well be upon him.

8) The policeman should not think of himself as an avenger, as a judge and executioner on the scene. His role is to apprehend and deliver a suspect to justice.

Are there ways to help the policeman in his mission to apprehend and ensure the safety of the suspect? Here is one suggestion. The policemen should be trained to be better shots. They should be able to shoot to harm without killing. Why is it that police departments utilize targets at the firing range that consist only of head and torso? Policemen do their target practice shooting at these lethal facsimiles of the body; they are not trained to shoot at the legs. When a fleeing suspect is unarmed, the policeman should hold his fire until he is closer and can ensure that he will hit nothing higher than the thigh.

Here is another suggestion. There are times when neither the Taser nor the gun is called for. What is wrong with using ropes, nets, lassos or gaucho bolas? If they work well against wild beasts, lions and tigers, running cattle and feisty broncos at a rodeo, they should work against a man. There are safe alternatives to the gun and to the Taser which are not being used.

In one recent case there were several policemen trying to apprehend a single man who was obese. There was no need to apply brute force, but they did –unimaginatively, like jocks on a football play, tackling, ramming through with brute force. This approach culminated in the death by chokehold of Eric Garner on July 17, 2014 in Staten Island, New York. The video of his apprehension was distressing and was made unforgettable by Garner's pleas, begging for help: "I can't breathe; I can't breathe." The man was heavy and couldn't have run to save his life. They could have easily controlled him with ropes and nets.

Another video of trigger-jittery police occurred in North Miami, Florida on July 18, 2016 when Charles Kinsey, a black mental health therapist was shot as he lay on the ground with his hands up. A few feet from Kinsey, sitting on the concrete, was his 23-year old autistic patient, playing with a toy truck. The video shows no imminent danger. Kinsey is calm, prostrate, unthreatening –always with his hands straight up in the air –as he explains to the police the circumstances. But suddenly out of the blue the policeman fires three shots, one of them hitting Kinsey in the leg. At least this time the shooting was not fatal. The episode ends with a dialogue between Kinsey and his shooter which is significant for its honesty. While the policeman was handcuffing him, Kinsey asked him: Why did you shoot me? The cop's answer was mystifying. He said: "I don't know."

We are reaping the consequences of sowing too many guns. There is nothing we can do about this in the short run. It would be madness at this point to suggest that the police disarm. I do not propose that. We are not ready for that. Perhaps thirty or forty years from now when we have changed the culture we could afford to reduce the arms involved.

For now it is enough to recognize that we live in a vicious atmosphere of inflamed fears which is caused by the gun and is fed by the gun. The gun has superimposed itself as an inextricable player in our lives and has wrested control from us by sucking us in its strong spiraling currents. The police cannot disarm because the criminals are armed; the criminals are armed because they need it for their nefarious business of intimidating victims and, also, because they need to protect themselves against competing gangs. Add to all this that it is much too easy to get guns and you feel the currents of the gun dragging us towards violence.

CHAPTER 17

Final Thoughts

• • •

ONE LESSON LEARNED ABOUT GUNS is that political apathy invites opportunistic lobbies to fill in the void and exploit it. They then push their ambitious agendas and prosper, growing into an empire that makes them lord and master of all aspects of the gun business.

But things are beginning to change. The demonstrations by the students from Parkland, Florida, have snowballed. First, they inspired other students in towns across the state; then they stirred students across the entire country, and then they moved people of all ages into action. Some gun owners felt so badly that they resorted to destroying their AR-15s, or turning them in to the police. Several corporations that included banks, insurance and car rental companies broke ties with the NRA.

This has been quite unprecedented. No other massacre has created such a widespread reaction. This school shooting has finally raised an enduring outcry that will not peter out until it gets real change. People are fed up with feeling like lambkins to the slaughterhouse. The fervor and resolve against the NRA and its political minions is unrelenting. The Florida students have taken their demand to the state capital and to Washington, D.C. They have made politicians of both parties take note. They have lit a fire that has materialized into a liftoff. Even I thought I saw a tremor on point B on the PP curve of Chapter 4 that made the curve quiver a bit. It prompted me to shout: Motion, we have motion at last!

As usual, pro-NRA politicians danced around the fire burning at their feet, spouting platitudes, dodging the issues and resorting to rhetorical pabulum about the victims being in their thoughts and prayers. In the past, people repressed their nausea at such hypocrisy and gave the politicians a pass. But this time the students expressed their disgust and held them to the fire. It has been gratifying to see the students keep up the pressure and demand real commitments for change here and now. Much of what I have heard –from both, the questions and the answers –is timely for this work and can serve as a recap and a conclusion to the book.

Background checks. Everybody talks about them and everybody is for them. But our background checks are full of leaks and are not broad enough. They need much work to be reliable. Compared to what other countries have in place, our umbrella of background checks is no more than a tattered rag over our heads.

I am critical of background checks, but not against them. We need them. But they need to be made stronger and their mission needs to be made firmer and clearer. Here are some issues to consider.

Who should implement the background checks? It should not be the gun merchant! His motivation is the sale of guns and does not have the interest of society at heart. The checks should be conducted by professionals, by law enforcement personnel who work in the best interest of the community and society in general. It should be a panel made up of individuals who are well versed in the business and who have degrees in criminal justice with a concentration in especial courses that have analyzed all the massacres of the last twenty years and know the failures of the previous cases so well that they carry their details on the tip of their tongues.

Where, in what building, should the background-checks be conducted? Not at the gun store! It should be in some official institution such as a courthouse or a police precinct, any place that lends solemnity and gravitas to the process. The prospective buyer should be disabused of the old notion that buying a gun involves only him and the gun vendor. He should know that society is in between and that it comes first. Basically, I am proposing a gun license.

Should the background checks include personal interviews? Absolutely! And not just one! The questioning would lengthen as more data becomes available and as officers read the application, depositions, police reports and other related documents. The applicant's response and reaction to his record could be very revealing.

Should the background checks include home inspection? Yes, but at the discretion of the panel. A professional woman who is applying for a handgun and who has no police record could be exempted. But it should be mandatory in the case of a high school student who wants to buy an AR-15. The professional woman is mature and can make a credible claim that her handgun is for self-defense. The teenager, by definition, lacks maturity and as a male has considerable statistical baggage. His application for an AR-15 calls for more investigation. His home is a good place to start. Do his parents know his intentions? Does he have other guns at home?

How long should the background checks take? This depends on the applicant's age, the type of gun, the applicant's gender, his immigration status and other conditions. If the preliminary checks raise questions, they may warrant further investigations and extensive field work that could take weeks. A young man who has made trips to trouble spots abroad would raise flags that should be pursued. A high school student, such as Nikolas Cruz, who has changed schools in his senior year because he was expelled in midyear, should definitely expand the field work. There is a story there which the investigators should research in depth.

It is important that people come to expect a lengthy process and not feel that they are being singled out for undue scrutiny. They should know that the days of quick automatic approvals for AR-15s are over. Americans should get used to the fact that the Second Amendment does not ensure swift purchases of AR-15s. They should respect the fact that society's priorities have changed, that security and precaution take precedence over half-vetted quick gun deals.

The time needed to buy a gun is a subtle indicator of what is wrong or right with a society. If it is too quick, as it has been in this country, it sends a bad signal, a wrong message. A loser, a rabid moron who thinks he can solve problems with a gun may believe that society actually abets him and accommodates him with his violent plans. He hears society tell him: "Go ahead, we won't hassle you; we'll help you get your equalizer and set you up with your justice-maker in not time. Here you go." On the other hand, if the process is protracted, the signal he gets is one of patience and counsel. He can almost hear society asking him: "Are you sure you need this? Do you think you are deserving of our trust? We need to study your request very, very carefully."

Much has been made of the fact that the FBI failed to act on a damaging phone call about Nikolas Cruz, the killer in Parkland, Florida. I concur that this is an egregious inexcusable fault of the FBI. It should be investigated and should be corrected so it never happens again. But this failure of the FBI was not the sole or main factor that facilitated Cruz's acquisition of the AR-15.

Cruz had so many issues that, had they been radioactive, they would have made Geiger counters chatter incessantly. You couldn't miss them. He was so blatantly at fault that a staff such as the one I have described above would have caught them easily and would have reacted swiftly. His application would have been put on hold from the start and would have given enough probable cause to inspect his home and confiscate his other guns. The massacre would have been averted despite the fumble of the FBI.

Of course, I am assuming that other laws would have been in place to support the background checks. The law I have in mind for this situation is the "red-flag" law which would have empowered the authorities to confiscate his arms based on the reports of his behavior and violent threats. A handful of states have such laws now. Rhode Island is the latest, having passed a bill which the governor signed just two weeks after the massacre in Florida. Score this as another vital consequence of the students' movement.

A license process that vets gun buyers on society's behalf does not need to be in a rush to sell guns, instead, it should be intent on smoking out those who would do us harm. Such a process would have caught most of the killers who flouted the current system. An effective system discourages, frustrates and ultimately foils would-be killers.

And yet, Republican politicians parrot the NRA line that such background checks don't work. They gainsay them and kill them on their say-so, without even trying them. Where is the proof that they would not work, if we have never had them? How can they be so imperious in their adamant denial? The simple answer is that for now they have the power. This is what needs to change. The gun problem in America is a political problem. Its ultimate solution is at the polls. For now the NRA has the votes, so the guns win at the expense of safety and human lives. Until this changes nothing of great consequence can happen. Even the student movement can fail before it in the short run. The NRA Republican politicians can up the ante by daring the protestors to remove them from office, if they can. So the real fight will be at the polls.

While the U.S. cannot show how effective real background checks can be –because we've never had them –other countries that have them, and are unhampered by Second Amendment or NRA blocking, can attest to how effective they can be. They bear out their results in terms of guns per capita and in terms of gun killings, which are much, much lower than here. Countries vary in their degrees of restriction. We need not be as stringent as Japan. There, virtually all guns are prohibited and the process to get a gun is an exercise in futility. Of course, because of that they have the lowest rate of gun deaths in the world.

Instead of background checks gun defenders love to offer their own cockamamie alternatives which, not surprisingly, call for more guns. They urge us to arm teachers and put armed guards in schools. That is overkill. They haven't even bothered to do the arithmetic. It means arming kindergartens, elementary schools, middle schools, high schools, colleges, malls and all places where crowds congregate. That is a staggering number of extra armed people.

It is also unnecessary because it is a second line of defense. It lets the killers get their guns and then gets ready for them. But if the license process is strong, which is the first line of defense, the second line is not needed. Arming the nation to the gills is not the answer.

Background checks can be much more effective than they have been, but they do have their limitations, which we should now consider. First, they do not catch the guns that are already out there. They work only on gun purchases and, obviously, the killers who have guns already do not need to buy them. There are also the unarmed but budding killers who can also bypass the purchase because they have access to dad's arsenal. This raises issues of gun control that are beyond background checks.

Second, background checks can't catch everybody every time. Some individuals arouse no suspicions; their application seems to be in the up and up. Paddock, the Las Vegas shooter, comes to mind. He seemed to be an upright citizen with no police record who gave no signs of trouble. He could pass the background checks –not only the ones we had in place then, but the ones proposed here.

To catch him we would have required a computerized system that kept tabs on his gun purchases and alerted the authorities. He aroused no suspicion because he was making purchases here and there. Each individual purchase was perfectly legal, but their totality smacked of nefarious intent. He beat the system by keeping his purchases apart in time and space. That should not happen again.

Actually, even the computerized system could not have prevented the massacre. We would have needed one more thing: a legal limit on the type and number of weapons that an individual can accumulate. What difference does it make that we are aware he is amassing deadly weapons if we can do nothing about it? This issue has not been broached yet. For that we need another law.

A license system is only a first step in a trek of hundreds of miles. We have far to go. Even a good license system is inadequate if it does not have the support of ancillary laws. Dozens of laws which do not yet exist would have to be passed and these laws, at present, have zero probability of being passed. The political temperament is inhospitable. Our gun idolatry is as deeply rooted and unshakable as an addiction, and this makes the fight for reasonable control of guns in 2018 quixotic and chimerical. The American people have to change the congress in elections to come. That will do it.

ABOUT THE AUTHOR

●　●　●

EDWARD ALBAN WAS BORN IN Ecuador but has lived in the United States and has been immersed in its culture for more than sixty years. He is a retired professor of economics with a body of published work, including a novel, a collection of short stories, and contributions to numerous literary journals.

www.ingramcontent.com/pod-product-compliance
Lightning Source LLC
Chambersburg PA
CBHW051315220526
45468CB00004B/1347